Women in Ministry

Women in Ministry

*Neither Egalitarian Nor Complementary: A New
Approach to an Old Problem*

JAMES B. DE YOUNG

WIPF & STOCK · Eugene, Oregon

WOMEN IN MINISTRY
Neither Egalitarian Nor Complementary:
A New Approach to an Old Problem

Wipf & Stock
An Imprint of Wipf and Stock Publishers
199 W. 8th Ave., Suite 3
Eugene, OR 97401
www.wipfandstock.com

ISBN 13: 978-1-60608-849-4

Manufactured in the U.S.A.

This book is dedicated to all the Christian women who have significantly impacted my life and convictions, including my mother, my wife, my sister, my daughters, missionaries, and students. They have graciously modeled the Lordship of Christ and have served well in his Kingdom. To God be the glory.

Contents

Introduction

The Debate Over the Role of Women in the Church

SEVERAL YEARS ago, a female student from China asked me what the Bible says about the veiling of women. Her pastor had recently asked her to wear a covering while attending a church in Portland, Oregon. She wanted to know if there was biblical warrant for her pastor's request.

As we together examined Paul's instruction in 1 Corinthians 11, we discovered that Paul's words did not mean that she should be covered when she participated in collective worship. In fact, it was just as much an error for her to wear a covering where it *is not* customary to do so as it was not to wear a covering where it *is* customary to do so.

Over the last few years, I've twice visited Afghanistan where the issue of the significance of a head covering for women is quite parallel to the biblical setting. I observed that most women cover themselves when in public. I also learned that women do not cover themselves at home or when in all-women situations (weddings, parties, and other occasions). Thus, in public, many wear a full covering, a *burkha*, of various colors that covers their entire body, leaving a small opaque panel in front of their eyes through which they may see. Others, especially in the capital of Kabul, wear a simple head shawl, called a *chadir*.

Interestingly, women in some modern Muslim states, such as the United Arab Emirates, often go without a covering at all, or wear the *chadir*, or wear a veil with the *chadir*. Thus there are variations within the same culture. These customs are meant to show proper deference to husbands, to shield their wives from other men.

I remember a particular instance of a young couple who apparently had recently married. I reflected on the fact that Afghan women usually adorn themselves with cosmetics and jewelry. Underneath her *burkha* she was probably quite beautiful. I remember thinking that it seemed entirely appropriate for this young husband to want to shield his new bride from the admiring, if not lustful, glances of men on the street.

What should a new female believer in such a land as Afghanistan do? Should she cover herself entirely, if her family or husband so demands, to follow the more conservative elements of her culture? Or should she feel free to disregard these influences of the culture and be uncovered now that she had become a Christian? Or should she conform to the culture in public but not in church?

There are other questions: As more liberalization comes to the culture, should Christian women be in the forefront of change? Most importantly, what guidelines does Scripture give to guide Christian women regarding this matter?

These questions are part of the larger issue of the role of Christian women in ministry, in the church in particular. In evangelical discussion and elsewhere, this issue has fallen for the most part into two schools of thinking—the complementary position and the egalitarian position.

The former affirms that while men and women are equal in their spiritual position in Christ they have differing divinely-ordained roles to play in society, including the church. In the church they may serve in various capacities, but not in teaching or leadership roles that place them in authority over men.

The latter, the egalitarian position, affirms that, because men and women are equal in their spiritual position in Christ, they should have equal roles in society, including the church. They may be able to exercise authority over men in the church should their gifting and calling equip them to do so.

This book seeks to bring another alternative to this debate between the complementary and egalitarian views. I suggest that the biblical view is neither complementary nor egalitarian.

Of the biblical texts that address this matter, three are primary: 1 Corinthians 11 and 14, and 1 Timothy 2. These are among the most difficult texts of the New Testament to interpret. This study seeks to interpret these to discover whether what they teach is universal, that is, still in force today.

The procedure is, first, to present significant background material to give a context for interpreting Paul's instruction. This consumes the first chapter. Then the three texts are examined in the next three chapters with special attention given to the question of universality. In the chapter on 1 Corinthians 14, I devote special attention to the thorny issue of what Paul means by his reference to "the law" in 1 Corinthians 14:34. I suggest a new idea for Paul's terminology.

Next, I devote chapter five to an examination of this question: If, in 1 Timothy 2:13–14, Paul makes an appeal to obvious universals—namely, the order of creation and the order of the fall, does this make his instruction universal or the normative thing for all time and places? I seek to show that within Scripture itself we can discover an example which suggests that the answer to the question is "no."

In chapter six, I introduce a new paradigm to discover what is or what is not universal. Such a paradigm brings together culture and history, the interpretation of the text, and theological truth derived from the larger context of Scripture. It brings together the contexts of culture, a text, and the canon. On the basis of this paradigm, I conclude that the role of women in the church is not universally fixed.

This study proposes that Paul's specific instructions regarding the dress and role of women in ministry is probably cultural and not universal in authority—true for all times and places. Even though Paul appeals to universal truth—such as the order of creation or the fall—this does not make the instruction universal. Special hermeneutical principles are involved.

Yet the context of culture prevents full realization of the equality of roles. The conclusion supports neither the complementary view nor the egalitarian view. Yet the promise of realization of full equality of roles is stronger than ever before in the history of the church.

Parallels Between Women's Life in Paul's Day and the Biblical Text

BACKGROUND INFORMATION FOR 1 CORINTHIANS 11

THE FOLLOWING is the text of 1 Corinthians 11:1–16 (modified from the NIV):

> Follow my example, as I follow the example of Christ. I praise you for remembering me in everything and for holding to the teachings, just as I passed them on to you.
>
> Now I want you to realize that the head of every man is Christ, and the head of the woman is man, and the head of Christ is God. Every man who prays or prophesies with his head covered dishonors his head. And every woman who prays or prophesies with her head uncovered dishonors her head—it is just as though her head were shaved. If a woman does not cover her head, she should have her hair cut off; and if it is a disgrace for a woman to have her hair cut or shaved off, she should cover her head. A man ought not to cover his head, since he is the image and glory of God; but the woman is the glory of man. For man did not come from woman, but woman from man; neither was man created for woman, but woman for man. For this reason, and because of the angels, the woman ought to have a sign of authority on her head.

> In the Lord, however, woman is not independent of
> man, nor is man independent of woman. For as woman
> came from man, so also man is born of woman. But
> everything comes from God. Judge for yourselves: Is it
> proper for a woman to pray to God with her head un-
> covered? Does not the very nature of things teach you
> that if a man has long hair, it is a disgrace to him, but
> that if a woman has long hair, it is her glory? For long
> hair is given to her as a covering. If anyone wants to be
> contentious about this, we have no other practice—nor
> do the churches of God.

REGARDING VEILS AND A WOMAN'S GLORY

Plutarch (*Moralia*, second century AD; written about Sparta, fifth century BC) notes that veils were a part of women's cloth-ing (21)[1].

Laws from the first century AD Rome allowed divorce if a husband caught his wife "outdoors with her head uncovered." The logic was that "the law prescribes for you my eyes alone to which you may prove your beauty . . . If you, with needless prov-ocation, invite the look of anyone else, you must be suspected of wrongdoing" (176). A husband could also divorce his wife for having a private conversation with a common freedwoman or if she dared to attend the games without his knowledge (176).

Aristotle (*Politics*, 1254b3–1277b25, etc.; Athens, fourth century BC) wrote regarding the difference between men and women: "All classes must be deemed to have their special attri-butes; as the poet says of women, '*Silence is a woman's glory,*' but *this is not equally the glory of a man*" (64; italics mine.)

REGARDING DISGRACE

Interestingly, the word "sin" rarely occurs in the Greek and Roman sources. Yet Paul's term, "disgrace" or "shame," does occur. A woman who practiced prostitution continued to bear "disgrace" even after she ceased to practice such. The occupation of a "panderer"[2] was not less "disgraceful than the practice of prostitution" (188). This text goes on to say: "*It is understood that disgrace attaches to those women who live unchastely*, and earn money by prostitution, even if they do not do so openly" (188; italics mine). "Disgrace" also attended a mother who formed a union with the slave of her son (196). This terminology suggests that Paul's use of the terms carries serious weight.

REGARDING WORSHIP
(THE FOLLOWING IS APPROPRIATE TO THE OTHER TEXTS AS WELL)

Regarding worship and clothing, Lucius Valerius argued for repeal of the Opian law in 195 BC. He pointed out that elegance, finery, and beautiful clothes were "women's badges in which they find joy and take pride." They put on for "public prayer and thanksgiving . . . still greater ornament" (180). He noted: "They prefer their adornment to be subject to your judgment, *not the law's*" (180; italics mine). This text also provides background for 1 Corinthians 14.

Participation in religion—in the form of rites, secret cults, orgies, trances, and magic—provided women the only justifiable purpose for meeting together (113). They were priestesses performing holy rites on behalf of cities and such deities as Demeter, Athena, Nike, and Apollo, as in Miletus and Athens in the third/ second centuries BC (113–118). There are epitaphs, inscriptions, and other sources (including letters) describing women's participating in orgiastic rites and what equipment they should have

(114). The *Homeric Hymn to Demeter* from the seventh century BC relates the story of Persephone and her return to her mother, Demeter, from Hades. Initiated women, especially those under sixty, could bring to the temple of the goddess the appropriate tribute (117). Women of all ages sought to appease the goddess Artemis, killer of women (118). Young women were to adorn their faces and their hair as gold in a ritual that marked their transition from girlhood to womanhood (119).[3]

Women also attended organized meetings outside the home for social or religious purposes—as burial societies or some sort of unofficial "ladies auxiliary" to keep feast days and honor the dead (244–245).

BACKGROUND INFORMATION
FOR 1 CORINTHIANS 14

The following is the text of 1 Corinthians 14:33–40:

> For God is not a God of disorder but of peace.
>
> As in all the congregations of the saints, women should remain silent in the churches. They are not allowed to speak, but must be in submission, as the Law says. If they want to inquire about something, they should ask their own husbands at home; for it is disgraceful for a woman to speak in the church.
>
> Did the word of God originate with you? Or are you the only people it has reached? If anybody thinks he is a prophet or spiritually gifted, let him acknowledge that what I am writing to you is the Lord's command. If he ignores this, he himself will be ignored.
>
> Therefore, my brothers, be eager to prophesy, and do not forbid speaking in tongues. But everything should be done in a fitting and orderly way.

REGARDING OBEYING HUSBANDS
(THIS PERTAINS TO 1 TIMOTHY 2 AS WELL)

According to a marriage contract from Alexandria, 92 BC, a wife is to remain with her husband, "obeying him as a wife should obey her husband, owning property jointly with him" (59).[4]

There is a surprising parallel to Paul's words in verse 35. In 195 BC, Rome passed the Opian law to curb women's use of expensive goods during a time of war. Twenty years later, the law was repealed after much debate. Conservatives complained that repeal would allow women to own gold, wear a "multicolored dress," and ride in a carriage in the city. Marcus Cato was blushed by women's behavior. They were "running around in public, blocking streets, and speaking to other women's husbands! Could you not have asked your own husbands the same thing at home? Are you more charming in public with others' husbands than at home with your own?" (177). In the past, women were not allowed to conduct any, including private, business without a guardian. They were to be under the authority of parents, brothers, or husbands (177). Cato went on to warn that *as soon as women became the equals of men they will have become their superiors* (178). The "womanish rebellion" sought to shine with "gold and purple," and would lead to women asking their husbands for money.

REGARDING SHAME

Plutarch (*Moralia*, second century AD) recounts an earlier tradition about the women of Miletus. An "insane impulse" led numerous young women to hang themselves. This malady seemed to be "of divine origin" until an ordinance was passed that required that those who hanged themselves should be carried naked through the marketplace to their burial. Since women could not bear the "thought of disgrace which would come after death," the practice immediately stopped. This is the "deterrent sense of shame" (97–98).

Yet others could write of a "covenant between man and wife; he must love her, always, until the end, and *she must never cease to do what gives her husband pleasure*" (19; from a speech in Menander; Athens, fourth/third centuries BC; italics mine).

REGARDING "THE LAW" REGULATING WOMEN IN WORSHIP, ETC.

The following sources show how important "the law" was in regulating marriage, worship, and virtually all of life. Roman law, though codified much later, had its roots in traditions from the eighth century BC Early laws are attributed to Romulus, the founder (753–716 BC). Such laws forbade putting children under three years to death, unless the child was a cripple or a monster from birth (173). Laws forbade patricide, and allowed the death penalty for adultery and for women who drank wine (175)—for "violating the laws of sobriety" (176). A wife who uses wine "closes the door on all virtues and opens it to vices" (176). Laws attributed to Numa Pomphilius forbade the burial of a pregnant woman before her child was extracted from the womb (174). A concubine who touched the Altar of Juno had to sacrifice, with "her hair unbound," a ewe to Juno. Other laws traced back to Romulus did not permit a woman to divorce her husband, but he could divorce her for the use of drugs or magic on account of children or for "counterfeiting the keys or for adultery" (173, 175).[5]

The law of Solon allowed that an adulterer may be put to death by the man who catches him in the act of adultery with his wife, and the one who does the killing shall not be found guilty of murder (44–45) (from Lysias, *On the Murder of Eratosthenes*; Athens, c. 400 BC). Whereas this law penalized seducers with the death penalty, rapists or violators were penalized only with a fine (45). In either case, the penalty was inflicted not in the interests of the people involved but in those of the whole community (47). Such laws were assumed to be an "inheritance from heaven" and the peoples' ancestors (47). To show pity for the victim rather than the murderer is the "far more just and more righteous course" for a jury "in the eyes of god and man" (49).

In a case brought against a former prostitute and adulterer (Appollodorus, *Against Neaera*; Athens, fourth century BC), the author cited the law to show the restrictions placed on a prostitute and an adulterer. The law decreed that she was forbidden to attend any of the public sacrifices "for the purpose of worship and prayer" (56). If she broke the law and attended the sacrifices, the law allowed any person who wished "to inflict upon her with impunity any punishment short of death" (56). The reason the law allowed this punishment was to prevent the pollution of the temple. The law held out for . . .

> women a threat terrifying enough to deter them from unrestraint or any sort of misbehavior, and compel them to carry out their duties at home, teaching them that if anyone misbehaves in this fashion, she will be banished not only from her husband's house but from the public places of worship (56).

The foregoing example perhaps helps us to understand why Paul thought so strongly about the proper manner of women's participation in praying, prophesying, speaking in tongues, etc., in public worship. Misbehavior could lead to the woman's banishment from both her home and from the congregation.

During this period, additional laws were enacted to protect marriage in various ways, although they favored the husband rather than the wife. The law codes sought to punish adultery, prostitution, and other immorality.[6]

In section 8 of his *Laws*, Plato asserted that the "unwritten law" of "public opinion" with the "backing of religion" would prohibit unnatural sexual intercourse and other challenges to "the law." He particularly sought to restrain and prohibit homosexual relations, "in which the human race is deliberately murdered," incest, and adultery. It was a "*natural* law" (75). Such a law recognized that such acts were "*absolutely unholy, an abomination in the sight of the gods, and at that nothing is more revolting*" (74; italics mine). He later identified the story that Zeus and Ganymede engaged in homosexual behavior to be a myth concocted by the Cretans to justify homosexual behavior among mortals (see also Josephus' witness to this in his *Against Apion*, II, 38; below).

The *Rules* of Ulpian (third century AD, Rome) considered women to be inferior. It was written: "Guardians are appointed for males as well as for females, but only for males under puberty, on account of their infirmity of age; for females, however, both under and over puberty, on account of *the weakness of their sex as well as their ignorance* of business matters" (193; italics mine). As shown below, this view of the inferiority of women characterized the whole period from the fourth century BC to the fourth century AD.[7]

In addition to Plato's recognition of "natural law" above, there was recognition of "natural law" among the Romans. The Justinian *Institutes* (sixth century AD) asserts that both "civil and natural law require that it [consent from relatives to marry] should previously be secured" (194). Thus, in "unions of the sexes, it should always be considered not only what is legal, but also what is decent" (194). "Marriage is dissolved by divorce, death, captivity, or by any other kind of servitude which may happen to be imposed upon either of the parties" (194). A true or actual divorce did not occur unless the purpose was to establish a "perpetual separation" (194).

The foregoing example is significant, pointing to the appeal to "natural law" which was common during Greek and Roman times, and which is found also in Paul. He appeals to what is "natural" (not only in 1 Corinthians 11:14–15 but in Romans

1:26–27); and his reference to "the law" here in 1 Corinthians 14:34 may refer to natural law (see below).

There is somewhat widespread understanding that some women were eloquent in speech. This would explain why some women would be capable enough to prophesy or to speak in tongues or to teach. From the first century BC and the first century AD come various accounts of how women were active in politics (even though they could not vote) and served as lawyers. They also were commended for bravery and courage in the face of national crisis (205–214).

Interestingly, "public law" prevented women "from participating . . . in Cybeline orgies in their homes," because such "forms of worship encourage drunkenness and ecstasy" (105). This is tacit acknowledgment that even pagan worship took place in homes, and not only in temples.

REGARDING THE WIFE'S HUSBAND AS TEACHER AND RELIGIOUS LEADER

Plutarch (*Moralia*; Boetia, second century AD) listed his advice to a newly married couple. Among other things, he talks about what plants will make her pleasant after "they have *veiled the bride*" (240; italics mine); it is the husband who leads and makes the final choice" (240); she should not be the one who initiates sex (240); she should not make her own friends, but enjoy her husband's; and the "first and best friends are the gods in whom her husband believes and to shut her door to all magic ceremonies and foreign superstitions. For no god can be pleased by stealthy and surreptitious rites performed by a woman" (240). The husband should be *"guide, philosopher and teacher in all that is most beautiful and most divine"* (241; italics mine.)

Menander wrote: *"The wife ought always to take second place in speaking,* and the husband ought in all things to take the lead. For there is not a home in which a wife takes first place which has not been utterly ruined"[8] (italics mine).

BACKGROUND INFORMATION
FOR 1 TIMOTHY 2

The following is the text of 1 Timothy 2:8–10:

> I want men everywhere to lift up holy hands in prayer, without anger or disputing.
>
> I also want women to dress modestly, with decency and propriety, not with braided hair or gold or pearls or expensive clothes, but with good deeds, appropriate for women who profess to worship God.

WOMEN'S CHASTITY AND CLOTHING

Regarding clothing, in Sparta during the seventh century BC, women were educated with full athletic training and all traces of effeminacy were removed, including "jewelry, cosmetics, perfumes, and colored clothing" (75). Spartan women "lord it over" the men (78). Children were the property of the whole commonwealth (77); and infanticide of ill-formed children (78) and abortion were practiced (79). Yet modesty and avoidance of shameful and licentious behavior were the goals (76–77). This situation in Sparta was recounted by Plutarch in *Life of Lycurgus* (14–16), written in the second century AD.

Dowries under Justinian (*Institutes*, sixth century AD) included sets of earrings described as "gold with genuine pearls weighing four quarters" and purple cloaks (199). Purple was made by a very expensive dye obtained from certain shellfish. "It was a sign of luxury. The togas of magistrates and wealthy youths ... were adorned with a purple stripe" (203, n. 12; see also 6).

Offerings to deities such as Artemis included embroidered and silken clothing, purple and green robes, tunics and cloaks, perforated earrings, gold rings, golden ornaments, and golden chains (120–121).

Regarding chastity and adornment, Socrates, according to Xenophon (*Oeconomicus*, 7–10, fourth century BC), believed that "the god directly prepared the woman's nature for indoor work and indoor concerns" while men were prepared for outdoor work and challenges (101–102). Some women thought that they could better please their husbands by applying cosmetics to their faces and makeup to their eyes, wearing high shoes, displaying counterfeit money, and by wearing necklaces of gilt wood and purple robes. Yet a wife's looks "become attractive" when "she gratifies her husband willingly instead of serving him under compulsion" (103–104). Gold jewelry and purple robes were indicators of wealth (as found as early as the sixth century BC in the poetry of Sappho) (6).[9]

Plutarch (*Life of Tiberius Gracchus* and *Life of Gaius*, Gracchus, second century AD) recorded that Tiberius chose to die for Cornelia, his wife, because she was such a "discreet" matron, "affectionate" mother, and a "so constant and noble-spirited" widow (139).

Seneca praised his mother, Helvia (in *On Consolation*, 16; AD 41/9), as set apart for her virtues. He wrote: "Unchastity, the greatest evil of our time, has never classed you with the great majority of women" (140). She was not impressed by jewels, nor pearls; she did not defile her face "with paints and cosmetics"; and did not fancy the "kind of dress that exposed no greater nakedness by being removed." People saw in her "that peerless ornament, that fairest beauty on which time lays no hand, the chiefest [sic] glory which is modesty" (140).

The concern for apparel was reflected later in the third century. There is mention made of a "women's senate" under Emperor Elagabalus (AD 218–222) which issued "absurd decrees" concerning what kind of clothing each matron might wear in public, who might ride in a chariot, and other particulars, including who "might wear gold or silver on her shoes" (246).

Tacitus writes similarly (*Dialogue*, 28; late first century AD). Rome's greatness was the result of its citizens' sons being the children of a chaste mother and elderly kinswomen of "approved and esteemed character" who never spoke "an unseemly word" or did a "disgraceful act." They regulated a boy's studies with "scrupulous piety and modesty" (141).

REGARDING DEVOTION TO HUSBANDS AND CHASTITY

The following is the text of 1 Timothy 2:11–15:

> A woman should learn in quietness and full submission. I do not permit a woman to teach or to have authority over a man; she must be silent. For Adam was formed first, then Eve. And Adam was not the one deceived; it was the woman who was deceived and became a sinner. But women will be saved through childbearing—if they continue in faith, love and holiness with propriety.

In Rome during the first century BC, inscriptions were made to praise women for their chastity, modesty, and devotion to husbands. Of one, it is written in the first person: "I was chaste and modest; I did not know the crowd; I was faithful to my husband" (134). On another tomb in Rome (c. 27 BC/AD 14), a son recorded that his mother deserved greater praise than all others since "in modesty, propriety, chastity, obedience, wool-working, industry and honor she was on an equal level with other good women, nor did she take second place to any woman in virtue, work and wisdom in times of danger" (136). From the third century AD, a freedwoman is praised on a tomb for being "courageous, chaste, resolute, honest, a trustworthy guardian." She "remained virtuous because she never committed any crime" (137). A statue from Lycia, first century AD, praises Lalla as "priestess of the Emperor's cult and gymnasiarch out of her own resources, honored five times, chaste, cultivated, devoted to her husband and a model of all virtue, surpassing in every respect. She has glorified her ancestors' virtues with the example of her own character" (157). This is typical of many statues and inscriptions (157–160).

The historian Valerius Maximus (*Memorable Deeds and Sayings*, first century AD) chose three women as examples of womanly virtue. Loyalty to a husband seems to have been the "highest excellence a woman could attain" (145).[10]

Writers often made the connection between chastity and clothing. In Italy during the third and second centuries BC, a treatise of the Pythagorean community in Italy asserted that "a woman must be good and orderly—and this no one can become without virtue . . . A woman's greatest virtue is chastity. Because of this quality she is able to honor and to cherish her own particular husband" (104).

The author went on to assert that, contrary to some people, he believed that men and women have in common such qualities as "courage, justice and intelligence" (104). Such chastity is learned and obtained by, most importantly, being pure in "respect to her marriage bed" (as well as by keeping her body clean, leaving her house in the proper manner, refusing to participate in the secret cults or Cybeline rituals, and by showing readiness, and using moderation, to sacrifice to the gods) (104). To commit adultery is to wrong the true gods of her family and to wrong her fatherland; and there is "no means of atoning for this sin" (104). "The greatest glory a free-born woman can have—her foremost honor—is the witness her own children will give to her chastity towards her husband" (104). The adornment of such a woman should include only white, natural, plain clothing; not transparent or ornate or silken material. She should not wear "gold or emeralds at all" nor apply imported or artificial coloring to her face; by washing only with water, she can "ornament herself with modesty" (105). They should not leave the home at night or in the evening, but at midday "to attend a religious festival or to make some purchase, accompanied by a single female servant or decorously escorted by two servants at most" (105).

REGARDING THE INFERIOR NATURE AND UNEQUAL ROLES OF WOMEN.

Regarding the inferior nature of women as understood in Greece, Aristotle (*Politics*, 1254b3–1277b25, etc.; Athens, fourth century BC) believed that *the female is inferior; the male is by nature fitted for command; and inequality is permanent* (64). Regarding household management he wrote:

> A husband and father rules over wife and children, both free, but the rule differs, the rule over his children being a royal, over his wife a constitutional rule. For although there may be exceptions to the order of nature, the male is by nature fitter for command than the female, just as the older and full-grown is superior to the younger and more immature . . . Nevertheless, when one rules and the other is ruled we endeavor to create a difference of outward forms and names and titles of respect . . . The relation of the male to the female is of this kind but there the inequality is permanent. (63–64)

He goes on to say that the deliberative faculty is absent in slaves, is immature in children, and, while present in women, it is "without authority" (64).

Regarding the moral virtues, Aristotle writes that, while all partake of them, they do so "only in such manner and degree as is required by each for the fulfillment of his duty" (64). The "temperance of a man and of a woman, are not, as Socrates maintained, the same; the courage of a man is shown in commanding, of a woman in obeying" (64).

Aristotle lamented the failure of Sparta to curb the licentiousness and luxury of women, so that:

> . . . the citizens fall under the dominion of their wives
> . . . But what difference does it make whether women
> rule, or the rulers are ruled by women? The result is the
> same . . . We are not, however, considering what is or is
> not to be excused, but what is right or wrong, and the
> disorder of the women, as I have already said, not only
> of itself gives an air of indecorum to the state, but tends
> in a measure to foster avarice. (65)

Plato (*Republic*; Athens, fourth century BC) advocated a new society where women would share some of the responsibilities for governing. Women would be nurtured and educated equally with men. Yet he held to the "general inferiority of the female sex: although many women are in many things superior to many men" (67). He believed that, while the "gifts of nature are alike diffused in both; all the pursuits of men are the pursuits of women also, but *in all of them a woman is inferior to a man*" (68; italics mine). In the new society, lighter tasks will be assigned to women "who are the weaker natures" (68). The best of either sex should be united in marriage to produce the best offspring; deformed infants and offspring of "inferior parents" must be killed, whereas the offspring of good parents were to be nurtured to become good parents. Incest was to be forbidden; and the offspring of incest were to be aborted (71).

Plato (*Laws*, fourth century BC) deals with how to promote a virtuous society. Sections 6, 7, and 8, deal with the greater role that women should play in society, that women should be educated, and that unnatural sexual intercourse should be discouraged and outlawed.

In section 6, Plato affirms that the female sex is "inclined to be secretive and crafty, because of its weakness," and that a "woman's natural potential for virtue is inferior to a man's, so she's proportionately a greater danger [to the state]" (72).[11] Plato laments the fact that his proposal for greater equal treatment of men and women is unpopular, that "at present, unhappily, the human race has not progressed as far as that" (72). Plato advocates that women should eat and drink in public, partake in communal meals as men do, yet because they have gotten use to a "life of obscurity and retirement . . . any attempt to force them into the open will provoke tremendous resistance from them" (72).

In section 7, Plato acknowledges that his proposal to educate both men and women equally, to give them a position of equality in Athens, is "incompatible with the average state's social structure" (73).

REGARDING WEAKNESSES IN WOMEN IN PROCREATION

Regarding the origins of the desire for procreation, Plato (*Timaeus* 91, fourth century BC) said, regarding male sowing in the womb, that it was "as it were plucking the fruit from the tree" (82). Aristotle (*On the Generation of Animals*) affirmed that male semen "effects generation" while the female semen, the menstrual fluid, "effects nutrition" (84). Hippocrates (*On the Generating Seed and Nature of the Child*, 4–7, 13, 30) on Cos, fourth century BC, asserted that both men and women produce male and female sperm, and the stronger sperm results in a male child, *whereas the weaker sperm results in a female* (87).[12] In his treatise *On Virgins*, Hippocrates believed that as "a result of visions, many people choke to death, more women than men, for the *nature of women is less courageous and is weaker*" (italics mine). Virgins, because of irregular flows of blood in their lungs and hearts, are more susceptible to experiencing visions and dreams than men, and this explains why *women more frequently experience hysteria and insanity* (96–97). The cure for this is to have sex with men, and *if "they become pregnant, they will be cured"* (96; italics mine). Sterile married women also are more likely to suffer the same end.

REGARDING THE MAKING OF WOMAN

According to Hesiod (*Works and Days*, Boeotia, early seventh century BC), various gods took part in the making of woman. Hermes put "lies, tricky speeches, and a thieving heart" in her breast according to Zeus' plans (13). This woman, called Pandora, removed the lid from her jar and scattered about all the evils that plague men—evils, harsh labor, cruel diseases, and miserable sorrows for men. Before this, men lived on earth without such evils (13).

One satirist, Semonides (*On Women*, Amorgos, sixth century BC), after citing all the beasts from which women are made, said that "this is the worst plague Zeus has made—women" (16). Zeus bound men to women "with a fetter that cannot be broken. Because of this some have gone to Hades fighting for a woman" (16). As the famous quotation from Hipponax (Ephesus, sixth century BC) has it: "The two best days in a woman's life are when someone marries her and when he carries her dead body to the grave" (16).

OBSERVATIONS

Paul's statements regarding practices of women are paralleled in the non-biblical literature of the day. Some assert that such material is useless because of the differences and diversity involved.[13] Yet the material does show the scope or range of customs involved.

Also this background material may inform us of the knowledge that Paul assumes his readers have. For example, in 1 Corinthians 11 he refers to "traditions" and "customs" that go unexplained. Since the text does not give us this information, we must seek to get it from other sources. This pursuit constitutes the pursuit of the context of culture.

It is interesting that the number one concern of the culture was the chastity of women. This is highlighted by the prohibitions against adultery, prostitution, incest, and homosexual behavior (which are brought together by Plato in the sources cited above).

The parallels in the secular literature suggest that such regulations in Paul are cultural and not universal and a standard for all times and places. However, one could argue that the parallels underscore the transcultural nature of the regulations. Yet this position is harder to maintain for the following reasons.

People living at the time did not view the regulations as final and unchangeable. For example, Plato himself advocated changes in various customs to bring about greater equality (as seen above). Also, changes did take place in the law (consider the reference to the Opian law above and Cato's response). In addition, Paul explicitly refers to these matters as "traditions" (1 Corinthians 11:2) and "customs" (11:16), and "laws" (1 Corinthians 14:34 and its reference to "the law" will be discussed below) rather than "revelation." Finally, changes began in Paul's day and have taken place over the course of time and differences have existed in different cultures at the same time.

One should note that, whereas women were often considered inferior and subordinate to men/husbands, opportunity for them to participate and even lead in worship did exist. From the literature of the day, there is evidence of such female participation or leadership taking place in Greek, Roman, and even Jewish culture.[14]

ENDNOTES

1. All the page numbers in parentheses in this part of the paper refer to Mary R. Lefkowitz and Maureen B. Fant, *Women's Life in Greece & Rome: A Source Book in Translation* (Baltimore: Johns Hopkins, 1982). There are other such sources that would add to what is here, and I cite some of them.

2. "The crime of pandering is included in the Julian law of adultery, as a penalty has been prescribed against a husband who profits pecuniarily by the adultery of his wife; as well as against one who retains his wife after she has been taken in adultery" (184).

3. The worship of the god Dionysus spread through Italy and appealed to the lower classes and slaves. It was characterized by orgiastic rites and secrecy, which to the Romans was a threat of sedition. In 186 BC, decrees were issued forbidding places devoted to the worship of Bacchus, any man or woman being a "master" of such an organization, and all rites conducted in secret or public without local permission (251). An assembly involved more than five persons. To violate these decrees was a capital offence and the places devoted to the worship of Bacchus were to be dismantled (252).

In worship of the god Asclepius, sterility was cured by "incubation"—sleeping within the temple precinct. If a woman saw a vision of a god in a dream, she would be miraculously cured (121) (from Epidaurus, fourth century BC). Such practice was also associated with the Egyptian god Serapis (123–124).

Women served as the six vestal virgins of the goddess of the hearth, Vesta. This cult began under the pious second king of Rome, Numa Pomphilius (715–673), and was described by Plutarch in the second century AD (249).

4. Following an annulment of a marriage contract, a woman is allowed to remarry and "expose" her baby born from the first marriage (fr. Alexandria, the Berlin papyrus 1104, first century BC) (60).

5. Women did have the right to inherit property but their place came after that of men and was restricted (36–37). Female children could inherit under certain conditions such as there being no male children (37). Yet "the law" expressly forbade "children and women from being able to make a contract" (38; in Athens, fourth century BC).

The Twelve Tables codified the ancestral laws on twelve bronze tablets in the Roman Forum. These were the basis of Roman civil law, arising in 450 BC While the laws became outdated they were never abolished (175). Table 4 provided for the immediate killing of a deformed child; table 6 stipulated that a woman who is "unwilling to be subjected . . . to her husband's marital control" shall absent herself for three successive nights in every year (175).

6. The law especially sought to protect marriage. Some law codes gave a husband the right to kill his wife if she were taken in adultery, but the law did not allow the wife to do such if the husband engaged in adultery or indecency (175).

In 18 BC, the Emperor Augustus sought to raise morals and the numbers of the upper classes in Rome. He enacted laws to encourage marriage and having children, and laws against adultery. The latter (*lex Julia de adulteriis coercendis*) punished adultery with exile and confiscation of property. Husbands could kill adulterers; they were required to divorce adulterous wives. Wives could not divorce their husbands, nor bring criminal accusations for adultery against them. Laws also punished the "detestable wickedness of women who prostitute their chastity to the lusts of others" (183). Although years later the laws were softened by *lex Papia Poppaea* enacted in AD 9, they were never formally repealed (181). Under Justinian (sixth century AD), the *lex Julia* was expanded to define adultery even more comprehensively (over five pages of stipulations are cited, 184–189). For example, one was punished as an adulterer if he lent his house to enable debauchery or adultery to be committed there with a "matron who is not his wife, or with a male, or who pecuniarily profits by the adultery of his wife, no matter what may be his status" (184–185). A woman could even be prosecuted for adultery after the death of her husband.

In a text (from Justinian, *Digest*; sixth century AD) somewhat reminiscent of Romans 7:1–3, regarding the freedom to remarry, it says: "If the adulterer should be acquitted, a married woman cannot be accused, even by the person who prosecuted the adulterer and was defeated, nor can she be accused if she should cease to be married, for the law only protects a woman as long as she is married" (186). Earlier, Plutarch (*Moralia* 288–9; second century AD) had written that a second marriage is to be deprecated, "for women are ashamed if they take a second husband while the first husband is still living" (242). It seems that Paul's regulation in Romans 7 in reference to the "law" could as much be a reference to contemporary civil law as to the law of Moses. Certainly his Gentile readers would recognize in their own laws the parallel with his words.

The concept of *patria potestas* is "the power of the father over his own family, which was a fundamental principle of Roman law" (including the laws given in the Twelve Tables) (189).

7. Yet, a wife differed from a concubine. Paulus, *Opinions* (third century AD, Rome) stated that a man "cannot keep a concubine at the same time that he has a wife. Hence, a concubine differs from a wife only in the fact that she is entertained for pleasure" (193).

8. Cited by Jerome D. Quinn and William C. Wacker, *The First and Second Letters to Timothy* (Grand Rapids: Eerdmans, 2000), 225. Regarding death, someone wrote: "For a female, death before marriage was considered particularly wasteful" (10, n. 9). Martial (*Epigram* 8. 12; Rome, first century AD) wrote of the disadvantages of having a rich wife. A rich wife is a husband not a wife. Instead, she should stay "beneath the husband; otherwise woman and man can't be equals" (242).

9. Regarding housing, men's quarters and women's quarters were apparently separated from each other in a Greek house, with the men's being downstairs and the women's upstairs (although a wife would sleep with her husband) (according to Lysias, *On the Murder of Eratosthenes*; Athens, c. 400 BC).

10. Wealth was often cited as a cause of unchastity. Cicero (*Pro Caelio* 13–16; 56 BC) faulted a woman who was pushing the prosecution of his client. He accused her of "affairs, amours, adulteries, Baiae, beach-picnics, banquets, drinking-bouts, songfests, musical ensembles, and yachting-parties." She "lived loosely, being forward, lived wantonly, being rich, lived extravagantly, being prurient, lived like a harlot" (149).

Juvenal (*Satire* 6; second century AD, Rome) satirized women. He asked where such "monsters" came from, and answered that the men and women of his day were the result of luxury and wealth. Whereas poverty made Latin women chaste "in the old days," money was identified as the "nurse of promiscuity" (154). Wealthy women avoided childbirth; they used drugs to make themselves sterile or induced themselves to "kill *human beings*" [italics his] in the womb. If these women did produce offspring, it would probably be "an Ethiopian . . . a wrong-colored heir" that the father would have to rear (155).

11. The view that women were inferior to men was reflected in the area of medicine. Galen (*On the Usefulness of the Parts of the Body*; Pergamum, second century AD) asserted that the female is "less perfect than the male" for one principal reason—she is colder. Among the animals the warm one is the more active, the colder animal is less

perfect than the warmer. It is so among people. A second reason for her being less perfect derives from her generative parts: because of her being colder, her generative parts could not project on the outside, while the man's could (215). He is "complete in all respects." However, the female is necessary for the propagation of the race. Galen went on to say: "you ought not to think that our creator would purposely make half the whole race imperfect and, as it were, mutilated, unless there was to be some great advantage in such a mutilation" (216).

Inequality between the sexes was experienced when children were young. For example, alimentary grants (cash grants for food) from governments or individuals "were customarily larger for boys than for girls" (243). Interestingly, there seems to be no place in the New Testament where boys are preferred over girls in Christian households and rules.

12. Pliny the Elder (*Natural History* 7; Rome, first century AD) wrote about pregnancy and the causes of abortion, which may be fatal in some cases. Fatal abortions are more likely when done in the fourth and eighth months of pregnancy. Abortions can be caused by sneezing following copulation, and the smell of lamps being put out (218).

Soranus (*Gynecology*; Rome, first century AD) wrote regarding the controversy over abortion. One party following Hippocrates refused to prescribe abortives and thought it better to prevent conception from taking place than to destroy the fetus. The other party prescribed abortion, to prevent subsequent danger to the mother, but not in cases of adultery or to preserve youthful beauty (221). Soranus went on to describe the many abortive agents and exercises that could be used to bring about abortion, including "wormwood" (222—224). He also opposed the theory of the "wandering womb" (228–230). Galen suggested that the primary causes of hysteria are psychological (231–232).

13. Gordon D. Fee, *The First Epistle to the Corinthians* (Grand Rapids: Eerdmans, 1987), 508–509, n. 70, discounts all such material as "generally useless" since ethnic, geographical, temporal, domestic, religious, and economic differences and diversity were all involved.

14. Note the examples in the literature cited above. C. Kroeger, "Women in Greco-Roman World and Judaism," *Dictionary of New Testament Background*, eds. Craig A. Evans and Stanley E. Porter (Downers Grove: InterVarsity, 2000), 1279, notes that a woman in Judaism was known to be an elder, "leader of the synagogue" and "mother of the synagogue" in Rome and Asia Minor. Greek and Roman

women served as priestesses, especially in the cults (1280). In the worship of Dionysius, "liberator of women," women were especially involved in the orgies. A woman's shrill, wild cry (called the *olulugia*) characterized several oriental cults. Rome had its Vestal Virgins (noted above from *Women's Life*), and women led in the worship of the Roman emperors (1280).

2

The Interpretation of 1 Corinthians 11:1–16

IT IS important to place the teaching about women in 1 Corinthians 11 in its biblical context. In the preceding context (1 Corinthians 8–10), Paul deals with rights or privileges which Christian may exercise but which they give up performing for the sake of the gospel. Believers have liberty or freedom (8:9; "authority, power" are other possible translations of *exousia*) to eat food sacrificed to idols, but they give up this freedom so as not to become a hindrance to the weak (verses 1–12), to wound their conscience and sin against them and so against Christ, or to cause the weak believer to sin.

SHOULD UNCOVERED WOMEN PRAY AND PROPHESY IN CHURCH?

In 1 Corinthians 9:1ff., Paul deals with his own "freedom" (verse 1) and his rights to financial support and to be married. He even cites Old Testament Scripture as supporting his right to have material support (verses 1–12). Yet he has not used this "right" (verse 12) and instead has endured everything so that he would not be a hindrance to the gospel of Christ. He determined to be free from all people so that he could become a slave or servant to all (verse 19ff.), whether to Jews under the law, or to those without the law, or to the weak, or to all people, so that he might save some. He does all these things because of the gospel. He exercises self-control, as an athlete, in order to receive an imperishable crown (1 Corinthians 11:23–27).

In chapter 10, Paul warns his readers to avoid the sins of the Israelites and to receive their history as instructive (1 Corinthians 10:1–11). God is able to deliver every one of his readers from temptation and provide deliverance (verses 12–13). He warns them of idolatry and participating in idol feasts (verses 14–22).

Then Paul proceeds to more neutral things. In the final verses of the chapter (10:23–33), Paul deals with the broad principles of edification of others as a concern to override one's rights (verse 23); seeking the good of others and not one's own (verse 24); "freedom of conscience" (verse 29); being able to give thanks for something as a test for freedom to indulge (verse 30); doing everything for the glory of God (verse 31); giving no offense to Jews, Gentiles, or fellow Christians (verse 32); and pleasing others not oneself, by seeking the benefit of others, not oneself, for the purpose that they might be saved (verse 33). He concludes, "just as I also try to please everyone in all things. I do not seek my own benefit, but the benefit of many, so that they may be saved. Be imitators of me, just as I am of Christ" (10:33–11:1).

This same spirit of freedom qualified by concern for others continues in 11:2ff. The concern for the limitations of liberty and "rights" continues the theme begun in 1 Corinthians 8:1 and continues into chapter 11. This is an important point to remember as one tries to decide whether the regulations regarding the dress and demeanor of women during church are universal—standards for all time and places—or temporary and culturally limited.

Some general observations are in order regarding 1 Corinthians 11. In these verses, Paul deals with what he calls "traditions," not "sins" or "transgressions" (verse 2). To violate what Paul writes would constitute a violation of tradition but not a violation of God's law or morality. Avoidance of shame is the governing concern in the passage because it was such in the culture of the day. Recall from chapter two, above, how often the concern for shame is mentioned in the secular literature of Paul's era.

THE MEANING OF THE HEAD COVERING

Paul's focus is on the need for women to wear a covering. Whether Paul refers to a veil, a covering, or a combination thereof, is unclear. Probably different forms were used even within the same local culture. The only imperative or command given in all of verses 2–16 (apart from the imperative, "judge this" in verse 13) is for women to keep wearing the covering or veil (verse 6: "let her cover her head"). The context deals with what is disgraceful in custom regarding having or not having long hair, and how the wearing of the veil or covering reflects this custom (verses 4–10). The shame seems related to a woman's becoming like a man in her style of hair, becoming "mannish." This suggests that the women at Corinth were blurring distinctions between men and women, especially sexual distinctions.[1] It is possible that the "covering" refers to a particular, loose style of hair, but this is less likely.[2]

In this text, Paul gives many reasons why women should be covered: Uncovered women bring disgrace to men/husbands (women's "heads") (verses 2–5); an uncovered head is like being shorn, which is disgraceful (verses 5–6); woman is the glory of man (verse 7); woman came from man (verse 8); woman was created for man (verse 9); she should exercise control of the authority, the freedom, of her head, because of the angels (verse 10); woman is not independent of man (verse 11); it is improper for an uncovered woman to pray to God (verse 13); long hair, like a covering, is her glory, not a disgrace, as it is for man, and accords with nature (1 Corinthians 11:14–15); and having a covering accords with the custom of the churches (verse 16).

It is important to note that Paul does not enjoin women to begin wearing veils or coverings when they pray and prophesy but to keep wearing veils when they do such. The difference is that Paul uses a present imperative in the Greek rather than an aorist imperative (verse 6). The former means that one should continue a practice; the latter usually means that one should initiate a practice not already in place. Evidently, Christian women thought that in an intimate relationship with God, such as praying and prophesying, their coverings could be removed. The thought is that the vertical dimension should trump the horizontal relationship. They had Paul's own words regarding equality in Christ (Galatians 3:28) to encourage them.[3]

In addition, the fact that in her own home a woman, a wife, was not veiled raised a problem: What does she do in her home when visitors come and engage in worship? Paul is concerned about the reaction of men and others, and so enjoins the continuing of the custom of being covered at all times when in public—even though the worship is taking place in a home. Yet what should a woman do if only women are present? The literature of the time (as shown above) shows that women could gather, among other reasons, for religious purposes. Thus when a woman's home became a church it was like "going out in public," and they as respectable women should wear the appropriate attire.

UNIVERSALISMS

Certain statements in this text are universals. These include the statements that Christ is the head of every man, and that man is the head of every woman, and that God is the head of Christ (verse 3); that man should not have his head covered "since he is the image and glory of God, but the woman is the glory of man" (1 Corinthians 11:7); that "man did not come from woman, but woman from man" (8); that man "was not created for the sake of the woman but woman for the sake of the man" (9); and that "for this reason a woman ought to have authority on [over] her head because of the angels" (10). The NIV renders these last words as: "the woman ought to have a sign of authority on her head."

The meaning of several of these phrases is disputed. One of the most difficult words to define is that of "head." It has been argued that the meaning of "the head of" is "the source of," "the authority over," or "pre-eminent over."[4] It seems to me, in light of the discussion cited in the endnotes, that the term has the general sense of "prominent" or "preeminent." This more general meaning allows all the different contexts of creation, culture, and equality in Christ (Galatians 3:28) or the gospel to impact the total meaning. In other words the total context (Scripture, culture/history, and theological identity in Christ) is given its full force. The different contexts all contribute to meaning, to the understanding of this text.

Since both men and women could pray and prophesy, the words of the text probably refer to men and women rather than husbands and wives (Thiselton[5] and most commentators agree). Yet the mention of veils presumes that Paul is dealing with married women in particular who gather for worship. Thus I think that there is greater support for "husbands" and "wives" than most allow. The assumption is that the people who gather are married. Blomberg observes that it is harder to understand "how Paul could have claimed that every man is an authority over every woman and much easier to interpret the passage if husbands and wives are meant throughout."[6]

The phrase, "because of the angels," is also difficult to grasp.[7] It seems that this refers to the presence of angels whenever Christians are gathered together to worship. They are "ministering spirits" for believers (Hebrews 1:14). Thus obedience to Paul's instruction about women worshipping would commend the worship of all.

The idea of "keep [have] authority on [over]" probably has the sense of referring to the outward symbol of a woman's inward deference to men, hence "authority" is often rendered "symbol" or "sign." While a woman has freedom to choose what to wear (perhaps a claim actually made at Corinth), in light of being created for man (verse 9) and "because of the angels," she should exercise this freedom in the proper way—"by maintaining the custom of being covered."[8]

THE QUALIFIERS

Yet these statements are qualified by other universals for Christian men and women. In 1 Corinthians 11:11, Paul says, "But in the Lord neither is woman without [apart from, independent of] man, nor is man without [apart from, independent of] woman." This verse introduces "more universal universals" for the Christian. The *plen* (πλην) suggests the idea of "nevertheless," "however," or "in any case" to break off a discussion and to emphasize what is important.[9] Note how "in the Lord" (at the beginning of verse 11) and "from God" (at the end of verse 12) bracket this verse as significant. It should qualify everything in this section (verses 2–16).

"In the Lord" means that one believer cannot exist without the other. In the new relationship, men and women are totally interdependent, living "out the life of the future, awaiting its consummation."[10] The sentence is meant to qualify a woman's claim to be able to exercise her "authority" or "freedom" (verse 10).

In any case, whether 1 Corinthians 11:10 is translated as the claim of the woman herself or Paul's own exhortation, verses 11–12 are meant to qualify any sense of inferiority that the woman/wife may feel in light of the created order and culture. After appealing to creation and culture, Paul now appeals to what it means to be "in the Lord." It is a claim parallel to the affirmation of Galatians 3:28: "There is neither Jew nor Greek, there is neither slave nor free, there is neither male nor female—for all of you are one in Christ Jesus."

The theological significance of being in Christ in the new creation is now added to the considerations of creation and culture. Somewhat akin to this is the idea, expressed by Thiselton, that "in the Lord" is an appeal to the gospel, that the gospel doesn't abrogate gender differentiation, but that in the gospel, differentiation "is determined more explicitly by a principle of mutuality and reciprocity. *There could be no reciprocity or mutuality unless each was differentiated from the other*"[11] (italics mine).

While this is true, this idea doesn't go far enough here. Thiselton takes "in the Lord" as meaning "among the Lord's people." He acknowledges that this principle, as the verse says, is reflected in the everyday experience of birth. Yet birth is experienced by all, whether in the Lord or not. I suggest that the gospel calls for an actualization of heaven's reality on earth where men and women have, as much as possible, equal roles. "In the Lord" means, as it does often elsewhere, "in Christ," in union with him. Thus we are drawn to Galatians 3:28 again. Bruce (107) sees it this way and comments: "since they are 'one in Christ Jesus' (Galatians 3:28), neither has higher dignity than the other before God, the author of all things." Barrett (255) says it is not simply "in the realm of the Christian life" but perhaps means "in the Lord's intention"—in the original creation and in its restoration. Blomberg (216) observes that the "nature of creation is substantially qualified but never erased altogether" by these verses.

In other words, what transpires "in the Lord" now that Christ has come was anticipated in the pronouncements of Genesis 1–3. We are to read and interpret Genesis in light of 1 Corinthians 11:11–12 and Galatians 3:28. The interpretation of Genesis is not complete or final apart from consideration of the New Testament texts.

To substantiate this statement (note how *gar*, "for," in verse 12 parallels the use of *gar* in verses 8–9), Paul says, "For just as woman came from man, so man comes through woman, but all things come from God." These words include both women and men, and sexual differentiation and procreation.[12] The stimulus for this affirmation may be Paul's assertion in 1 Corinthians 8:6: "But for us: one God, the Father, from whom all things come and we go unto him, and one Lord, Jesus Christ, through whom all things are and we [go to God] through him." Verse 12 prevents the text, including verse 3, "from being read in a subordinationist way."[13] In Christ men and women are interdependent.

Note how verse 12 counters the statement of verse 8, or gives the "other side of the coin." Identification with Christ makes a difference or acts as a qualifier to Paul's previous statements. If verse 12 counters verse 8, then it may also counter verses 3 and 7. While verses 7–12 teach that "the distinction between male and female must be maintained," there is no support here for the subordination of women to men.[14] Men and women share a common nature. The new order in the Lord is one of equality.[15]

In 1 Corinthians 11:13–15, Paul returns to the specific concerns (found in verses 4–6) of women praying and prophesying without a covering. Yet he seems to expand the covering to include a woman's hair itself. Since women have been given "by nature" long hair as a covering,[16] this in itself argues that they ought to be covered when praying or prophesying. Apparently, then, wearing a veil or covering reflects their hair covering. Again, Paul refers to what is "proper" (πρεπον) and "disgraceful" (ατιμια), not to what is "sin" or "transgression" of some rule or law.

Paul's appeal to "nature" (verse 14) is "not an appeal to Nature, or to 'natural law,' or to 'natural endowment'; nor is Nature to be understood as pedagogic (actually 'teaching' these 'laws')."[17] It is a question of propriety, custom, or disgrace. Paul gives no theological significance to "nature." Hence the thrust of "nature" is "the nature of things" (NIV), the "way things are," the "natural feeling" that people shared "together as part of their contemporary culture."[18] It points to the "regular order of things."[19] Interestingly, what "nature teaches" here, Fee observes, comes about by "unnatural" means—by a haircut![20]

Finally, Paul once more reminds his readers that it is "custom" (συνηθειαν) to which he is appealing (verse 16). Most see the passage as culturally limited. It does suggest that from culture to culture certain modes of dress are appropriate and others are not.

Thus Paul, after proceeding through culture, creation, and theology, ends up on culture or custom. Culture has been his concern regarding Christian freedom throughout chapters 8–10. Christians are free to do all sorts of amoral things (what they eat or drink or wear or not wear), but they should not indulge their freedom if exercising it brings slander against the gospel as people see their culture being violated. While Christians are "not of the world," they should be perceived as "of the world." [21]

ENDNOTES

1. Fee, *Corinthians,* 511. See his footnotes (67–85) supporting this breakdown in sexual relationships or distinctions.

The view of gender distinctions is well argued by Benjamin L. Merkle, "Paul's Arguments from Creation in 1 Corinthians 11:8–9 and 1 Timothy 2:13–14: An Apparent Inconsistency Answered," *JETS* 49/3 (Sept. 2006) 527–48. The "apparent inconsistency," which egalitarians raise, arises from the observation that in both passages Paul argues from creation that women should wear veils when praying and prophesying (1 Corinthians 11) and that they should not teach or exercise authority over men (1 Timothy 2). Yet almost everyone agrees that the wearing of veils is a cultural matter and can be rejected today, while the prohibition of teaching or exercising authority over men should be affirmed. Is it not inconsistent to reject the former practice while affirming the latter when Paul bases both in creation? Merkle's resolution of this dilemma is to assert that the former instruction regarding a veil is only indirectly related to the argument from creation, since Paul's chief concern is to preserve "gender and role distinctions" and the wearing of veils only upholds this distinction as a particular application which could change in other cultures. In the second text, the prohibition regarding teaching and authority is directly tied to creation, and "therefore is transcultural" (528). Merkle (534–36) cites five reasons based in verses 7–9 for why the main concern of the passage is gender and role distinctions.

The point of my study is to question this last conclusion. I also think that Merkle fails to deal with certain issues. For example, how today is gender distinction upheld? In addition, others take the view that the primary issue is coverings or veils (see below). It is significant that Merkle's position is not explicitly stated by Paul; he does not say that gender distinction is the issue at heart. Also, Merkle seems to overlook the significance of verses 11–12 that seem to counter Paul's strong statements by reminding the readers how it is "in the Lord." These words clearly call forth a remembrance of Galatians 3:28. Finally, Merkle gives virtually no mention of the concept of shame and why it appears.

Merkle and others believe that the Corinthian women were taking off the veil to symbolize their rejection of gender distinctions because they had embraced an "over-realized eschatology" and an "over-emphasis" on the Spirit and spiritual gifts (528). This situation came about because they had taken Paul's teaching regarding the *eschaton* too far. They believed that the kingdom had fully come; it was "here" and no longer "not yet." They had fully embraced the teaching that Paul himself had affirmed in Galatians 3:28. Merkle makes a strong case from within the text of 1 Corinthians for this possibility, citing at least nine examples of how the Corinthians had an "over-realized" eschatology (529–32). Others extend this to the men at Corinth as well—they were not dressing appropriately (533, n. 24).

Merkle (534) finds that Paul gives three arguments for maintaining gender and role distinctions: he argues from creation (verses 7b–9), from nature (verses 14–15), and from practice (verse 16). Interestingly, he does not cite the argument based in what is shameful (e.g., verses 4–6, although this is cited in verse 14) and what is proper (verse 13).

My view is that Merkle and others are correct, that believers at Corinth and Ephesus had an "over-realized" eschatology. Yet Merkle and others have not applied Galatians 3:28 enough. They have a stagnant view of the "here but not yet" paradigm, when it should be ever unfolding (as in the case of slavery). They have an "under-realized" eschatology. I return to this concern near the end of this book.

2. Fee, *Corinthians*, 509–10; n. 71–78. Richard B. Hays, *First Corinthians* (Louisville: John Knox, 1997), 185ff., takes it as having the hair tied up or bound rather than hanging loose.

Ben Witherington, *Conflict and Community in Corinth* (Grand Rapids: Eerdmans, 1993), 232, says that the issue is head coverings; to affirm hairstyles is beside the point. The issue is head coverings for both men and women in worship; only those actively doing the worship were to wear it, not all (234). He argues for the cloak or *himation* that was pulled over the head, not a veil, hair, or other head covering (237).

Thus there is not a consensus on the matter of head "covering" but this issue is not crucial for the purpose of this study (as will be seen).

David E. Garland, *I Corinthians* (Grand Rapids: Baker, 2003), 518, also argues that long hair suggesting effeminacy or sexual ambiguity is not the issue but the matter of head coverings is. Uncovering the head had sexual implications (520); respectable women avoided drawing attention to themselves. The veil or hood "constituted a warning" that no man should dare approach her without suffering penalties (521). Uncovered women in public "gave nonverbal clues that they were 'available'" (521). Paul's primary purpose is to prevent women from becoming "objects of attraction to be sized up" by men during worship (521). Such behavior would reflect poorly on the men in her life—her husband or father or other male relatives (522)—and bring them shame before God when she should be their glory. "The man stands uncovered because he reflects the glory of God; the woman must be covered because she reflects the glory of man" (523). Women need to "project modesty and virtue in their dress" (522), as in 1 Timothy 2:9ff. The veil signifies that the woman is chaste and modest and devoted to her husband and intends to stay that way (509–10; note the same in the secular literature cited above). Garland quotes Derrett as saying that "the husband's rights are not forfeited simply because their spiritual status is changed by their conversion" (510). This goes to the heart of the issue—why women may have been prone to take off the veil in worship.

Merkle ("Paul's Arguments from Creation") rejects Garland's view as not weighty enough to explain Paul's extended response based "on God's design in creation" (533). Yet Merkle's response seems to be too subjective.

3. This view of the situation is less profound than that of Merkle ("Paul's Arguments from Creation") and others who find that the chief problem was failure to keep the gender distinctions of Galatians 3:28. The women thought that such distinctions were erased now in Christ. I'm suggesting less. The issue is also the wrong understanding of equality in Galatians 3:28. Yet it did not lead women to erase gender distinctions but to remove the veil during the exercise of spiritual gifts. This removal of the veil would bring slander against the gospel from men and more conservative women. If gender distinction is the issue, it seems that men who would be prone to pursue gender identity go unaddressed. Also, a woman without a veil still keeps gender distinction by her long hair. It seems that making the issue gender distinction goes too far and is unnecessary.

A strange use of Galatians 3:28 is that by Russell D. Moore, "After

Patriarchy, What? Why Egalitarians Are Winning the Gender Debate," *JETS* 49/3 (Sept. 2006, 569–76), who uses it to support patriarchy. He pleads for a return to a strong patriarchy to offset the feminism of our culture. He believes that the erosion of human patriarchy, of male headship in the home and in the church, in American culture stems from an erosion of the doctrine of God. The texts cited by egalitarians really prove patriarchy (including Galatians 3:28), he believes (575), since they point to a Father who has given His Son in whom all may be identified. This seems a bit of a stretch, exegetically. He too easily equates the egalitarian view with feminism, and the complementary view with the patriarchy of God.

4. The several major views of how to interpret the word "head" are strongly argued. (1) Fee (*Corinthians*, 501–5) and others take "head" as signifying "source" rather than "authority over" in light of the context. He discounts the research done by Wayne Grudem to support "authority over." "Source" is also the view of F. F. Bruce, *1 and 2 Corinthians* (London: Oliphants, 1971), 103; Raymond F. Collins, *First Corinthians* (Collegeville, MN: Liturgical Press, 1999), 405; and C. K. Barrett, *A Commentary on the First Epistle to the Corinthians* (New York: Harper & Row, 1968), 248–49. He finds that a "chain of originating and subordinating relationships is set up: God, Christ, man, woman" (249).

As Fee points out, in the context (1) the actual word for "authority" refers to the woman's (verse 10); (2) verses 11–12 are meant to point not to subordination but equality; (3) verses 8–9 resume the "woman . . . man" of verse 3 and in these verses source is the idea; and (4) the creation is the idea, as witnessed by verse 12 where woman comes from man and "all things come from God." Thus the verse points, not to subordination or hierarchy, but to relationship flowing from source. Christ is the source of every Christian man—a reference to the new creation; cf. verse 4 and Colossians 1:18 (rather than it being a reference to Creation and Christ being the source of all people); and God is the source of Christ at the incarnation. Yet verse 11 means that creation should be understood from "a Christian perspective" (so Collins, 412).

(2) A second view is that the term means "authority" or "chief." Hans Conzelmann, *1 Corinthians*, trans. James W. Leitch (Philadelphia: Fortress, 1975), 183–86, takes it as "chief" with subordination involved. While this appears to be invalidated by being "in the Lord" in verse 11, it isn't, he observes (190). Craig Blomberg, *1 Corinthians: The NIV Application Commentary* (Grand Rapids: Zondervan, 1994), 208–9,

gives several reasons why "authority" cannot be excluded from the idea of "head," and believes subordination is involved (as in Ephesians 5:22–24). Yet both subordination and mutuality of relationship are involved, and he cites the parallel with the functional subordination that Christ has to the Father (217). He also suggests that subordination, defined as a mutual submission, may be limited here to marriage (217–218). Hays, *First Corinthians*, 183ff., believes that "ontological preeminence" and "patriarchal implications" are involved; yet verses 11–12 counterbalance this by affirming that men and women are called to live as "complementary partners" and have a "functional equality" (188–189). Witherington, *Conflict* (238) takes it as "authority," yet verses 11–12 make it clear that while there is a hierarchy of God and Christ over humans, there is not a hierarchy of man over woman (Paul didn't practice such; Romans 16:7). Yet gender distinctions that God created remain (240); but leadership means servanthood in the inversion that Christ has brought (240). W. Harold Mare, *1 Corinthians*, in *The Expositor's Bible Commentary* (Grand Rapids: Zondervan, 1976), 255, cautions that, while the three cases of being under a "head" include authority, including a woman being under man's authority, Paul "does not mean by his analogy that subordination in each case is of the same completeness." This is wise counsel. Merkle, "Paul's Arguments from Creation," 535, supports the idea of "authority over," following the work of Wayne Grudem.

(3) Probably the best view is that defended by Garland, *1 Corinthians*, 505ff. He finds that it is not "source" (even without any hint of subordination there is little lexical support for this meaning), nor "authority," "supremacy," "ruler" or "chief," but the idea of "pre-eminent," "foremost" or "priority." In other literature, it has this basic meaning without links to ideas of obedience or submission. As Garland notes (516), the one in second place (here Christ and man) is not inferior to God and Christ respectively. Paul does not assert the subordination of women nor the supremacy of men. Rather he establishes that each has a spiritual head and what one wears either honors or dishonors one's spiritual head. Men who wear coverings shame their head, Christ. What a woman does "reflects upon the man who as her head is representative of her, the prominent partner in the relationship, or that the woman's status and value is summed in the man" (Garland, 516, quoting Perriman, 621). Charles J. Ellicott, *St Paul's First Epistle to the Corinthians* (London: Longmans, Green, and Co., 1887; rep. n.d.)

believes that the general idea is that of supremacy or pre-eminence, but the character of this must be determined by context (200).

Garland (513) observes that the text, even in verse 3, does not support the subordination and inferiority of women. For if she is in a lower position, why does she stand in the middle of the three statements, with God mentioned last? Paul is not giving a chain of command; instead references to Christ frame the statements about man and woman. (I would observe that this accords well with the idea that everything centers in Christ, including "all the treasures of *wisdom* and knowledge" [Colossians 2:3]). Garland (532) rejects a subordinationist Christology in verse 3; the issue is obedience.

(4) Another view is that expressed by Anthony C. Thiselton, *The First Epistle to the Corinthians* (Grand Rapids: Eerdmans, 2000). He argues that it is "inadequate" to construe the relationship within the Trinity as hinging only on obedience (803). It is neither egalitarianism nor an overstated "subordinationism" that explains Paul's view of God and of gender (804). As clear from Philippians 2:6–11, the relation of God-Christ is not "*an involuntary or imposed 'subordination,' but an example of shared love*. This shared love controls the use of freedom, and thereby each brings 'glory' to the other by assuming distinctive roles for a common purpose" (804; italics his). "Paul's concern is not with subordination but with gender distinction" (805). The text is about both "men and women, freedom, and *respect for the otherness of the other in public worship*" (805; italics his).

Thiselton argues that "head" is a word with multivalent meanings (803) and these interplay with the metaphorical applications. To fail to recognize this is the "most serious mistake of much exegesis" (803). It is a "*polymorphous concept*, through a word that has *multiple meanings*" (811). As Garland above, he turns from "source" and "authoritative headship" and prefers slightly the idea that "head" denotes head in contrast to body but more widely "that which is most prominent, foremost, uppermost, pre-eminent" (812).

In addition, Thiselton (803) points to the "seminal work" of Judith Gundry-Volf (1997) who suggests that neither egalitarian nor hierarchical interpretations "do justice to the complexity of the theological issue for Paul" (803). Both are involved. Paul always "superimposes" three frames of reference for gender relationships: the order of creation, society or culture, and the gospel (803). All of these need to be read into the text of chapter 11. Paul can appeal "to creation to support instructions which presume a hierarchical relationship of man and woman as well as undergird their new social equality in Christ without denying their difference" (Thiselton, 811, quoting Gundry-Volf). Thus if Paul asserts a "theoretical hierarchy," the one foremost within this hierarchy must protect the weaker for whom they must take responsibility (821), as chapters 8–10 show. Thus Thiselton translates 11:2 as: "I want you to understand that while Christ is preeminent (or head? source?) for man, man is foremost (or head? source?) in relation to woman, and God is preeminent (or head? source?) in relation to Christ" (800).

The traditions that Paul commends them for (verse 2) may well be those teachings concerning how both men and women may pray and prophesy, rather than the issue of coverings (811). I suggest that they also concern the matter of "male and female" being one in Christ; and this explains the "but" of verse 3.

5. Thiselton, *Corinthians*, 822.

6. Blomberg, *1 Corinthians*, 210.

7. "Because of the angels" may reflect part of the women's claim that they are like angels already—not given to marriage (see 7:1) and free; or that they spoke an "angel's language." Others point to Qumran literature that alludes to the presence of angels when the community is gathered; so Collins, *First Corinthians*, 412. Yet the exact meaning is probably lost (so Fee, *Corinthians*, 522). After weighing several explanations, Garland (*1 Corinthians*) decides that Paul assumes that angels are present "as observers and that their presence necessitates paying even greater heed to conventions of modesty" (529). He cites Luke 15:7, 10; 1 Timothy 5:21; Hebrews 1:6; 12:22–23. Christians worship the transcendent God "in company with the heavenly host" (Thiselton, *Corinthians*, 840–41). The majority of commentators (see also Barrett, 254; Witherington, 236; Mare, 256; Ellicott, 205–6; etc.) take this view. Some add to the idea of observance that of angels' being guardians (841) (so also Bruce, 106; Blomberg, 212; Hays, 188).

8. Fee, *Corinthians*, 521; and the NET Bible. This is virtually what Paul asserts in 8:9 (n. 31): "Be careful, however, that the exercise of your freedom does not become a stumbling block to the weak." Women should control their head by wearing the head attire proper to the culture (Garland, *1 Corinthians*, 525). The word for "authority" is εξουσιαν which is used several times in the preceding context, with such ideas as "liberty" or "freedom" (8:9) and "right" (9:4, 5, 6, 12 [twice], 18); and is interchanged with "freedom" (ελευθερια) and "free"

(ελευθερος) (9:1, 19; 10:29). This word establishes the common theme for all of chapters 8–14 (so Thiselton, *Corinthians*, 799). Love for the other qualifies "freedom" and "rights." The sense is that she is "to keep control of (how people perceive) her head" (Thiselton, 839).

Others enlarge on this idea. Bruce, *1 and 2 Corinthians*, 106, states that the veil was a sign of the woman's new authority; in Christ she received "equality of status with man; she might pray or prophesy at meetings of the church . . . Its ordinary social significance was thus transcended." This is also the view of Barrett, *Corinthians*, 255: the woman is veiled, for she reflects the glory of man. The veil prevents her from glorifying the male and allowing God to be glorified. Veiling prevents her from shaming her "head," man, 254. Hays, *First Corinthians*, 188, comments that Paul is telling the women to "take charge" of their own heads. The covering is a "fitting symbol of the self-control and orderliness" that the whole community should show.

Merkle, "Paul's Arguments from Creation," 536, n. 31, presents two reasons why it is better to think that Paul is here responding to a question from the Corinthians regarding the wearing of a covering. He supports the translation, "symbol of authority," and faults egalitarians for merely using the translation, "exercise authority" (537, n. 33). He cites Liefeld as agreeing with his view when Liefeld concludes that it seems difficult that Paul would conclude "with a statement that a woman can do as she pleases in this respect."

Yet this is not what Paul is saying. Rather, in effect he is saying that a woman should exercise authority over her head—she should give up liberty and rights and live by custom (in keeping with the whole theme of chapters 8–11). "Exercise authority" is the most straightforward translation.

9. *BDAG*, 669.

10. Fee, *Corinthians*, 523, n. 41.

11. Thiselton, *Corinthians*, 842 (italics his).

12. Barrett, *Corinthians*, 255.

13. Fee, *Corinthians*, 524.

14. Ibid. Yet Merkle, "Paul's Arguments from Creation," 538, believes that Fee is only partially correct and that one cannot separate insubordination from the act of casting aside head coverings. The latter was a rebellion against "God's created order" which put the "husband as the head" or in the "position of authority over his wife." Yet Paul's statements do not seem to address wives and husbands but women and men (even

though the word for "man" is ανηρ throughout and not ανθρωπος). Much of the complementary view is based on the idea that women and men are the focus of these texts, not just wives and husbands.

15. Collins, *Corinthians*, 403. He notes that there is "radical equality between men and women;" yet, Paul adds, men should look like men, and women should look like women.

16. Fee, *Corinthians*, 529.

17. Ibid., 527.

18. Ibid.

19. Ibid., 526, n. 12. Thiselton, *Corinthians*, 844–45, agrees with this definition, translating it as "the ordering of how things are." My own study of the term "nature" agrees with this definition; see chapter 4 in my *Homosexuality: Contemporary Claims Examined in Light of the Bible and Other Ancient Literature and Law* (Grand Rapids: Kregel, 2000). It is a "particular cultural code" (Hays, 189). However, Merkle, "Paul's Arguments from Creation," 535, disagrees and believes that the term "nature" refers to "God's design in creation (cf. Romans 1:26–27)." He cites Epictetus (a Stoic of the first and second centuries AD) as supporting this idea (535, n. 29). Yet it seems that Epictetus' remarks are not tracing the differentiation to creation but to birth, to the natural way people are.

20. Ibid., 527, n. 15.

21. Ibid., 530. Conzelmann, *1 Corinthians*, 191, says that Christians must "maintain the imperceptibility" of their "unworldliness" by wearing their hair normally and dressing normally.

3

The Interpretation of 1 Corinthians 14

A SIGNIFICANT part of the problem surrounding the role of women in ministry is the matter of the place where the church gathered for worship. They gathered in homes where women normally did not wear veils or coverings in front of their families. So when does a home become a church? Apparently it is transformed when others (neighbors, strangers, etc.), particularly men but also women, gather to pray, to prophesy (edify), and to express other spiritual gifts as a community (1 Corinthians 14:26: "*when you come together, each one* has a hymn or *a word of instruction*, a revelation, a tongue or an interpretation"; italics mine). At this point the norms of the culture regarding public meetings take over.

SHOULD WOMEN KEEP SILENT IN CHURCH, "AS THE LAW SAYS"?

The most significant point in this passage regards the problem of Paul's obscure reference to "the law" in 1 Corinthians 14:34. While the referent of Paul may be the Old Testament, there is no Old Testament source for his words. It is better to view Paul as alluding to secular law, not the Law of Moses or the Old Testament. As shown above, there certainly were parallels regarding women's behavior in public and in public meetings and cited as "the law" in the law codes of the day.

THE MEANING OF "THE LAW"
IN JOSEPHUS AND PAUL

Interestingly, Paul's words are paralleled by Josephus (in his *Against Apion*, 2.200–1), and this common usage argues that Paul's referent is to secular or natural law.[1] Both the meaning and the significance of this saying are interesting. Fee (*Corinthians*, 707) cites Josephus as reflecting Paul and quotes him as follows (from Thackeray in the Loeb series): "The woman, says the Law, is in all things inferior to the man. Let her accordingly be submissive."

The problem is that Josephus actually makes a fuller statement: "The woman, it says, is worse than the man in all things. Let her accordingly be submissive, not for her humiliation, but that she may be directed; for God has given the authority to the man" (translating εδωκεν as active, "has given," rather than passive, as Thackeray translated it). It is better to translate "woman" as "wife" and "man" as "husband," since Josephus clearly has wife-husband relationships in mind directly before and after this quote. In light of II.199, the "it" in "it says" seems to refer to the Old Testament Law, as a summary of certain marriage regulations: "The Law (ο νομος) recognizes . . ." In the earlier context, Josephus is in the process of detailing certain regulations from the Law, the Old Testament.

Yet between this statement beginning II.199 and that in II.200–1, Josephus cites tradition implied by the Talmud (see Loeb II, 373, ns. b, d) and not found in the Law at all. Fee points out that Paul may be appealing to an oral understanding of the Law such as found in a rabbinic formula (see n. 34, 707).

Fee and some others argue that this statement and verses 34–35 are a gloss or a scribal addition for two reasons. Nowhere else does Paul ever appeal to the Law without citing the Old Testament text that he has in mind; and the Old Testament does not say what he says it does. Barrett (333) slightly favors this view, as does Hays (246–48). The latter thinks that all attempts to explain these verses as a part of the text fail; yet since they are in it, they should be read (with 1 Timothy 2:12ff.) in light of Paul's wider vision of "men and women as full partners in the work of ministry" (249).

Yet most reject the idea that the verses are a gloss. Some find the source in Genesis 3:16 or in Numbers 12:1–15 (the incident of Miriam's questioning of Moses' authority), but neither of those texts says what Paul here says it does. Others suggest that these words are only summarizing the Genesis account, but this seems a bit of a stretch. Bruce (*Corinthians,* 136) believes that the reference is to the Pentateuch, specifically to the creation narratives, since 11:3ff. cites such narratives (this is also the view of Blomberg, 282).

Thiselton agrees but goes further. He believes that the verse points to the patterns of order shown in divine actions of creation "through differentiation and order" (1153). Hence, the imperative is rendered, "let them keep to their ordered place" (1155). The command is not to submit to husbands but to the principle of order (1155). This is not the submission of Genesis 3:16, since it would conflict with Galatians 3:28. It is part of the future resolution when all things (see 1 Corinthians 15:28), including Christ himself, will *"resume his ordered place . . .* in relation to the God who orders all things" (1155; italics his). Thiselton adds: "This exhibits an 'ordered' Trinity, not a 'subordinationist' Christology" (1155).

It seems far more simple to believe that Paul is citing culture as "the law" (note the secular parallels cited above), and this happens to agree with what rabbinic sources and Josephus also say (who also may be citing common law or culture). Barrett (331) goes further, believing that Paul is citing both Genesis 3:16 and "the common feeling of mankind."[2]

Thus Paul does not cite the Law of the Old Testament here, nor Josephus; but he is closer to Josephus. The Old Testament also does not say that women should be submissive (nor, hence, that they be silent in the churches and not allowed to speak). The mention of "authority" (*kratos*, κρατος) in Josephus seems to parallel Paul in 1 Corinthians 11:10 (*exousian*, εχουσιαν). Thus Paul's words have the authority of culture behind them, but not biblical (Old Testament) revelation. Even if the latter were granted, as regulations from the Old Testament, their authority for Christians is not assured.

ADDITIONAL SUPPORT FOR "THE LAW" AS CULTURE

There is more to support the view that Josephus and Paul are citing cultural laws or tradition—but tradition common to Jews and Gentiles. After the portion cited above (II, 201), Josephus cites "the law" as regulating, in addition to matters dealt with in the Old Testament, such things as bringing up offspring, forbidding abortion and infanticide, or exposure (note the parallel with secular law), since this labels a woman a murderer, and forbidding birthday parties. The law regulates funeral expenses, forbids monuments for tombs, and forbids the "revelation of secrets" and concealing "anything from friends." The law also prohibits setting the country on fire, cutting down fruitful trees, abusing women, and harming brute beasts.[3] Yet these things cited as coming from "the law" are not found in the Old Testament.

Yet another argument supports the referent as cultural law. Josephus (and Paul) view that all mankind, including the ancient philosophers, such as Plato, had special revelation from God. Therefore, cultural law that agrees with Biblical law is authoritative.

Josephus makes several claims regarding the extent that knowledge of the Jews, their beliefs, and their laws were known. Josephus argues that Plato and the wisest Greeks and others had the "same sentiments" as the Jews about the nature of

God (Book II, section 17, in Whiston's translation); that Plato's precepts were "pretty near to the customs of the generality of mankind" (section 32); that Plato himself confessed that he did not feel safe "to publish the true notion concerning God among the ignorant multitude" (section 32); that Plato and other philosophers "agreed with us as to the true and becoming notions of God" (section 37); that Plato "principally imitated our legislator in this point, that he enjoined his citizens to have the main regard to this precept, 'That every one of them should learn their laws accurately'" (section 37); that the Jews' laws have "always inspired admiration and imitation into all other men" (section 40); that the earliest Grecian philosophers "in their actions and their philosophic doctrines, follow our legislator, and instructed men to live sparingly" (section 40); and that "the multitude of mankind itself have had a great inclination for a long time to follow our religious observations" (section 40).

Josephus allows for no exceptions—whether among the Greeks, the barbarians, "nor any nation whatsoever"—where customs of the Jews such as Sabbath keeping, fasts and festivals, food regulations, etc., are not observed. All try to imitate their mutual concord of living together, their charity, trading, and fortitude. Their laws prevailed by their own force; and "*as God himself pervades all the world, so hath our law passed through all the world also*" (section 40, italics mine). The great number of those who desire to imitate the Jews' laws "justify us in greatly valuing ourselves upon them" (section 40). The piety of such laws means that the Jews have "become the teachers of other men, in the greatest number of things; and those of the most excellent nature only" (section 42).

Josephus is claiming that special revelation, like general revelation, is universal. Again, this is remarkably like Paul. In Romans 10:18, Paul cites Psalm 19:4, dealing with general revelation, to support the universality of hearing the gospel. Thus when Paul cites "the law" it does not matter if it be Biblical law or cultural law, for they are one when the latter agrees with the former.

This solution, taking the referent as secular law, mitigates the need to consider 1 Corinthians 14:34–35 as a gloss added to the text after Paul penned the letter.[4] The verses are an authentic part of the text.

Paul's concern is not for women and men in general but he is concerned that a wife not shame her husband, her head (11:3). In light of the secular texts cited in the first part of this study, and, in particular, the parallel in the quote from Cato, this view seems best.

Paul is dealing with what is shameful in culture, especially when wives would embarrass their husbands in their homes by contradicting them or questioning them over the scrutiny of prophecy (verse 29). It would be especially problematic if the wife was also a prophet or spoke in tongues (verse 26). With Garland (669ff.), it seems best to take the view that Paul is dealing with wives transgressing social norms for what should go on in a home that has become a church, where mixed participation of men and women occurred and raised questions regarding the relationships between genders. The silence is a temporary suspension of speech, not of all participation (as in verses 28 and 30), and does not contradict 1 Corinthians 11:5. The subjection does not imply inferiority of the wife but demonstrates her Christian love for her husband. Also, Paul may fear that the Christian community might be mistaken for one of the orgiastic, secret cults that Rome sought to restrain, as the secular texts cited above also show.[5]

THE DIFFERENCE BETWEEN PAUL'S VIEW OF WOMEN AND THAT OF HIS CONTEMPORARIES

The most interesting thing about Paul's citation of what "the law says" is that Paul skips the first part of the saying (as found in Josephus) that asserts that "a wife is inferior to her husband in all things." Instead he quotes or refers only to the next clause, the inference made from the first, which begins with "therefore" or "for that reason" (τοιγαρουν), that she should be submissive to him. This clause is not even part of what "the Law says" but an inference drawn from it.

Paul is deliberately avoiding any such statement about a woman's or a wife's being or nature and takes up the consequence regarding her behavior that flows from her being, her nature. This is indeed remarkable and clearly puts Paul in contrast to Josephus and to Philo ("woman is more accustomed to be deceived than man"; *Questiones in Genesis,* 1.33), and to secular law codes of the Greeks and Romans.

Significantly, it should be pointed out that never does any biblical text state that women are inferior to men, or that wives are inferior to husbands, as do the non-biblical texts. Whatever inferences may be drawn from the Biblical text that may seem to point in this direction, there are no texts that assert such. This suggests the intrinsic superiority of the teaching of the Biblical texts. There is always in the background Paul's great statements about the equality of men and women (or husbands and wives) in Christ (Galatians 3:28).

There were significant and differing results that came from how non-Christians valued women as compared to how Christians valued them. Because non-Christians aborted or exposed their daughters more frequently than their sons—most limited their daughters to one—there came to be an imbalance in the population. The ratio could be as high as 140 men per every one hundred women. But because Christians, following the teachings of Christ and of Paul, opposed abortion and infanticide, Christian women outnumbered men and held far more positions of influence and power in Christian circles. Also, Christian women more often represented first or primary conversions compared to men, who represented secondary conversions—they married female Christians.[6]

There is another point reinforcing the view that this passage is culturally limited. If Paul's appeal amounts to an appeal to "natural law," it is another similarity to his appeal to "nature," "the nature of things," as found in 1 Corinthians 11:14. This is parallel to non-biblical legislation, as cited above. For Paul here, and there, what is "natural" is culturally defined. This differs from "natural *moral* law" which concerns such things as homosexuality, incest, and adultery (as in Plato, *Laws*, cited above) and which are not culturally defined.

We should no more think that the regulations regarding the covering of women are transcultural than to think that Paul's limitation regarding the number who can speak or prophesy (limited to "two or at the most three," as seen in 1 Corinthians 14:27–29) is transcultural. No doubt this number was determined by the size of the congregation (a home with a courtyard could hold at most about fifty people) and by the length of the service. This observation applies to his other regulations in 1 Corinthians 14 as well.[7]

ENDNOTES

1. From the Loeb series, II, 373.

2. Paul's word for "submission" is υποτασσεσθωσαν; that of Josephus is υπακουετω. Interestingly, 1 Clement uses υποταγης of a wife's subjection to her husband: she is to "remain in the rule of obedience" (so Kirsopp Lake in the Loeb series: *The Apostolic Fathers*: [Cambridge: Harvard, rep. 1965], I.10).

3. These citations come from Book II, sections 25–30 in "Antiquity of the Jews: Flavius Josephus Against Apion," in William Whiston, *Josephus: Complete Works* (Grand Rapids: Kregel, 1960), 632.

4. There are two broad views regarding 14:34–35. (1) Fee, *Corinthians*, 699–705, and Conzelmann, *1 Corinthians*, 246, argue for an interpolation, while (2) Collins, *First Corinthians*, 515–17, and Witherington, *Conflict*, 288, argue for its being an authentic part of the text (it is a conservative argument that Paul opposes and rebuts by his double rhetorical question in verse 36). If it is an authentic part of the text as written by Paul, there

are several explanations. Garland, *Corinthians*, 665, reviews the main interpretations if it's not an interpolation: (1) it's a Corinthian quotation that Paul refutes in verse 36; (2) it's Paul's directions for husband-wife relationships in the church's public meetings; (3) it's Paul's directions for man-woman relationships in general. Garland decides for the second view (667ff.). Verse 35, with its mention of "their husbands at home," clearly supports this view. Even the idea of "let them be in submission" in verse 34 suggests a wife rather than a woman in general, for wives are to submit to husbands but not to every man in the church (cf. Ephesians 5:21–24; Colossians 3:18; 1 Timothy 2:11–15; Titus 2:5; 1 Peter 3:1–6). Others, such as Blomberg, *1 Corinthians*, while allowing for the view just described, suggest that these verses may better be viewed as limiting the ability of women to decide about the legitimacy of prophecy, which role was reserved for the elders or overseers, and they were exclusively men in the first century (281). Women could, however, engage in tongues, interpretation of tongues, and prophecy (the order of gifts just before).

5. Indeed, Witherington, *Conflict*, 287, suggests that Paul is opposing the assumption that Christian prophets or prophetesses functioned like the oracle at Delphi who only prophesied in response to questions. Paul argues that Christian prophets and prophetesses speak in response to promptings of the Holy Spirit.

6. For this information see Rodney Stark, *The Rise of Christianity: How the Obscure, Marginal Jesus Movement Became the Dominant Religious Force in the Western World in a Few Centuries* (San Francisco: Harper, 1977), chapter four.

7. Blomberg, *1 Corinthians*, 219, finds in these verses one of the clearest texts in support of women preachers. On the other hand, Mare, *1 Corinthians*, 276, takes Paul's command as absolute: Women are not to do any public speaking in the church. They were to be silent. Thus 11:5ff. may be understood as Paul's not saying that women were actually praying and prophesying in public worship (277). This seems an unlikely way to resolve the difference between chapters 11 and 14.

4

The Interpretation of 1 Timothy 2

THE MEANING of 1 Timothy 2 is one of the three most important texts (with 1 Corinthians chapters 11 and 14 as discussed in previous chapters) dealing with the role of women in ministry, and arguably the most difficult of the three to understand. In the following pages, I seek to deal clearly and carefully with the words of the text, and, in the process, I hope to bring clarity to the discussion of the issues involved.

SHOULD WOMEN TEACH OR EXERCISE AUTHORITY OVER MEN?

The following exegetical comments on 1 Timothy 2:12–15 derive from various sources, including articles and the following commentaries that support what is called the egalitarian view (Marshall, Liefeld, Oden, Dwight in Huther, 113; Dibelius and Conzelmann); those that support what is called the complementary view (Mounce, Knight, Arichea and Hatton, Johnson, Robertson, Fairbairn, Hendriksen, Barrett, Guthrie, Kelly, Liddon, Bernard, White [*Expositor's Greek Testament*], Ellicott, Huther, Chrysostom—as a result of the Fall; etc.); or those that support neither of these two views (Quinn and Wacker), or something else. Throughout this section, I've indicated where I differ from the views presented and given my own input. The numbers (1, 2, 3, etc.) are used to indicate separate matters of interpretation as they occur in the order of the text. They are used for purposes of clarification and reference only.

COMMENTS ON 1 TIMOTHY 2:12

(1) In the words, "I don't permit" (verse 12), Paul is making an authoritative assertion (Robertson), not simply giving a personal opinion (as Oden, 97, holds). The present tense and indicative mood don't detract from the fact that this is a "universal and authoritative instruction or exhortation" (Knight).

Yet it seems to me that while the words may be authoritative they may not be universal. A true imperative would have been a clearer indication of a universal (so Liefeld, 98). It may be considered a gnomic statement (Mounce, 122). The imperative of 1 Timothy 2:11 sets the tone of the verse.

(2) "To teach" (verse 12) means to teach religious instruction in the setting of the church (Liefeld, 98), which was also a home. It is basically equivalent to the function of the elder or overseer, yet it is not to be limited to barring women from such offices (Knight, 141). Paul could have simply said that women should not hold these offices. Paul is concentrating on the function, not the office. So he is prohibiting women "from publicly teaching men, and thus teaching the church" (Knight, 141). Yet it is not a prohibition of all instruction (Ellicott, 52). "Teach" contrasts "learn" in verse 11; the two verses parallel each other (Mounce, 123). Mounce suggests that the object of "to teach" is to teach doctrine to overseers in the church, since the opponents are teaching error (124); yet he acknowledges the difficulty of this view (125–26; Liefeld agrees that this is unlikely).

This suggests that women may teach men, even in an authoritative way, as long as they don't teach error. Is it possible for the overseers "to oversee" a woman teaching others, even teaching them, the overseers?

(3) The prohibition concerns the teaching of "men" by "women" (most interpreters: Johnson, Knight, Guthrie), although a strong case can be made that the people should be understood as husbands and wives (so Luther in Oden, 98;

Quinn and Wacker, 199, 223, citing Titus 1:6 and 1 Corinthians 14:33–35; perhaps Liefeld, 99; White, 108; Lock, 32), as also in 1 Corinthians 11 and especially in 14:34–35 (but see my discussion above). Quinn and Wacker (228) also point out that "Eve" in 1 Timothy 2:13 becomes "wife" or "woman" (γυνη) in verse 14, supporting the translation, "wife." Finally, only a "wife" bears children (verse 15), yet it is probably assumed that this is what women always do.

(4) The implication is that women "may not teach or exercise authority in or over the church" (Knight; consider 1 Corinthians 14:34–34; and 11:2, 16). Mounce (120) finds that the woman is to be subject, not to all men (in verse 11), but to teaching overseers; hence the context is public church meetings.

(5) The ουδε (verse 12) links "teaching" with "exercising authority" as a continuing idea (translated as "nor" or "or"). They are distinct but related concepts (Mounce, 129). The latter is a principle, the former is its application, as in verses 9–10: "teaching is one way in which authority is exercised in the church" (Mounce, 130).

Yet, I ask, why didn't Paul put the principle first followed by the application, which is the order in verses 9–10, where modesty is followed by examples or applications? What are other ways to express authority that Paul does not mention? It seems more likely that the idea goes from the narrower to the larger concept; or that the second clarifies what the first involves—teaching involves authority. Marshall (460) points out that the word characterizes the teaching not the role of the women in the church in general, and he gives it a negative sense (see below).

(6) The infinitive αυθεντειν is the second complementary infinitive after "I do not permit." As a rare term it may mean (a) "to have or exercise authority" (Knight, 14; Mounce, 130), a positive idea; or (b) a negative idea such as "to domineer" or to teach "in a domineering way" (Oden, 97; Guthrie, 76; Robertson, 4:570; Huther, 105; Bernard, 48; Ellicott, 52–53;

White, 108; Lock, 32; Arichea and Hatton, 58 [who also define "submission" in 1 Timothy 2:11 as including "recognition, subordination, and obedience"]).

Some argue (Liefeld, 99) that the word is stronger than "to have authority" but not as strong as "domineer"; so it may mean "to boss" (Quinn and Wacker, 200–1). This meaning refers to exercising leadership in the church, which is the function of the office of elder or overseer (Liefeld, 99, opposes this). Johnson (201) finds its meaning in opposition to "subject" and thus refers to women reversing the power structure. Mounce (128) finds here a prohibition of any type of authoritative teaching that would put a woman over a man.

(c) A third view of the term is presented by Marshall (458), who accepts Kostenberger's findings that the two terms ("teaching" and "exercising authority") must both be either positive or negative. The context mentions the deception of Eve and this must point to some particular false teaching by women, some of whom were vulnerable and being victimized; see 2 Timothy 3:6–7 (so Liefeld, 104). Thus the teaching and the exercising of authority are judged negatively and disapproved, contrary to Kostenberger, Knight, and Mounce. Rather than "to be in subjection" (verses 12 and 11), women were given to an "exuberant and excessive flaunting of freedom in the face of men," perhaps because of an "over-realized eschatology" taught in Corinth and Ephesus (consider 1 Corinthians 15:2; 2 Timothy 2:18; etc.) (Marshall, 459; so also Kelly, 68). Thus, whether or not αυθεντεω in itself "is pejorative, it is the exercise of authority *over men* which is the problem, so that the whole phrase is pejorative" (Marshall, 459; italics his).

I think that this is the best view. The "flaunting of freedom" assumed from the context here is parallel to the need for women in 1 Corinthians 11:10 to "control their freedom (their authority) over their head."

(7) In contrast (note the αλλ) to these functions, women are "to be in silence" (verse 12). Note that she is also to "learn in silence in all subjection" (verse 11). These words seem to exclude all types of authoritative teaching (Knight, 142). Yet the emphasis on "in silence" contrasts the "teaching and exercising authority" especially if the latter is negative (see Marshall, above). Oden (97) takes the object of submission to be God, not men.

COMMENTS ON 1 TIMOTHY 2:13

(8) The "for" (γαρ) is causal, giving the reason for the preceding prohibition (so almost all interpreters). The "for" is not illustrative—that Eve merely illustrates a woman who was deceived by Satan (so Liefeld, 100). Mounce (130) says that the creation order "indicates that God intended male authority" and that the "specific application of this principle" is that "Ephesian women should not try to reverse the created order by being in authority over men." Mounce finds this as "somewhat the same argument as in 1 Corinthians 11:8–9," yet he acknowledges that Paul "clarifies himself" in verses 11–12 (130).

Yet earlier Mounce (and others) argued that the application is more narrow than this—it refers to teaching men who are in positions of authority in the local church. On the other hand, why cannot the principle be applied to all of life—to domestic, civic, governmental, and other institutions? Why should Paul extend "male authority" beyond the family (its sense in Genesis 2) to the church? And if 1 Corinthians 11:11–12 "clarifies" 1 Corinthians 11:8–9, why should it not do so here? Why should we not read "in the Lord" here, to "clarify," i.e., to "qualify" this instruction? There (in 1 Corinthains 11) proper dress and roles and "headship" were addressed. Is not this text parallel to that? If it is, then "in the Lord" as a qualification would mean that there may be some churches where greater equality could be exercised because greater overall maturity prevailed.

(9) Paul's words in 1 Timothy 2:13 mean that he appeals to the entire creation narrative of Genesis 2—not just the chronology of it, but what this chronology entails, as shown in 1 Corinthians 11:8–9 (Knight, 143: Verse 13 is a terse statement of 11:3ff.). Yet, I observe, then the implications drawn in 1 Corinthians 11:11–12 are also involved.

Others suggest that what is "chronologically prior is taken to be in some sense superior" (Kelly, 68; Guthrie, 77; Bernard, 48; White, 109). Yet this has no bearing on the essential reality or identity of women. The timing of woman's creating has no bearing on how one defines what a woman is.

Others observe that what Paul does is similar to what Jesus does regarding marriage (Matthew 19:4–6) (Knight, 143). Yet I would suggest that the cases are not parallel. Adultery is a matter of morality and identified as sin by the Ten Commandments. Women authoritatively teaching men is never identified as transgression, sin, or immoral.

Johnson (201) finds Paul's appeal to creation to be equivalent to 1 Corinthians 14:34, "just as the law says." Yet above I argued that this verse refers to cultural law, not the Bible. Oden (99) significantly observes that the order of creation is not a statement of superiority or inferiority (or subordination?) but a statement of completion—that Eve completes what was incomplete in Adam, what was his limitation. He is the head, she is the crown. She was made from his side "to be equal with him" (quoting Matthew Henry).

COMMENTS ON 1 TIMOTHY 2:14

(10) Verse 14 is another basis with verse 13 for what Paul says in verse 12. The "and" (και) suggests that verse 14 is a second reason parallel to verse 13 for what Paul says in verse 12 (so Mounce, Marshall, etc.). The structure is parallel to verse 13. Yet Knight (144) takes it not as another basis but as an example added to verse 13.

Paul's appeal in verse 14 is to the events of Genesis 3. Eve was deceived, not Adam. The fact that Paul uses "woman" instead of "Eve" as he did in verse 13 is probably due to the use of "woman" in the LXX (the Greek translation of the Old Testament) account of the temptation (Knight, 144). It also allows Paul to use Eve as a type of all women; hence the order is from "Eve" to "woman" to "women" in verse 15 (Knight, 144). Yet it is possible that Paul is thinking here of "wife" again.

(11) The compound form of "was deceived" (εξαπατηθεισα) used of Eve (1 Timothy 2:14) is probably a stylistic variation of the term (ηπατηθη) used for Adam. It is unlikely that the term has sexual overtones, as in later Jewish reflection. It is significant that Paul uses the same term of Eve in 2 Corinthians 11:3 in a warning to all believers, men and women, at Corinth.

The role of verses 13–14 in respect to the prohibition regarding women is highly debated. This is a crucial issue. (a) They are a comment on the nature or ontology of women in general—as though women are more open to deception (note the secular and Jewish literature cited above; so Guthrie, 77; perhaps Huther, 107, 109, 113; Fairbairn, 129–30; Liddon, 19; Kelly, 68–69; Bernard, 48; Doriani, etc.); or that women are intellectually inferior (White, 109). Yet this view is unlikely in light of 2 Corinthians 11:3, where Paul uses the example of Eve's being deceived as a warning to all the believers at Corinth, not just to the women or men.

(b) They may be showing what happens when "roles are interchanged and women take leadership" (there is ontological equality but functional subordination). Hence the text has a universal significance (Mounce, 137, 139; so Barrett, Moo, Schreiner, Hurley, etc.).

(c) It seems best that the verses point neither to ontological inequality nor to functional inequality (so Fee, Payne, Keener, Kroeger, Marshall, etc.). Fee argues that the point Paul makes is not about Adam but about Eve's deception, since it is addressed or elaborated on in 1 Timothy 2:15. While this text prohibits women from teaching men at Ephesus, it is a unique text and not intended to correct the rest of the New Testament (cited by Mounce, 141–42). This view tends to dismiss the words, that "Adam was not deceived," a point of concern for Mounce.

Yet these words may be a case of *litotes*—Adam was deceived, he did sin, but not in the sense of Eve, the only one about whom deception is recorded in the text and is Eve's own admission. Liddon (19) suggests that it is a case where the silence of Scripture is "often as full of meaning as its assertions" (he cites Hebrews 7:3). Yet it is an error for Mounce (142) to state that the same limited restriction/application could be placed on Galatians 3:28. No one doubts the universality of Galatians 3:28.

Of special note is the entire absence in 1 Timothy 2 of some such statement as found in Galatians 3:28 that all are one "in Christ Jesus" (consider "in the Lord," 1 Corinthians 11:11–12). Yet I argue that the text here needs the qualifier, "in the Lord," in light of the larger context of Paul.

Finally, the proponents of the (b) view have to make so many qualifications regarding the nature, the recipients, and the location of the teaching intended in verse 12, without specific statements in the text itself, that the view becomes suspect.

The overriding basis for the universal significance of the passage is the appeal to creation. Yet such an appeal does not necessarily make the instruction universal, as I will show in the chapters that follow. In addition, Paul's point is the deception of Eve, not her insubordination (Liefeld, 100). Chrysostom held that the subordination of woman, defined as lacking authority, began at the Fall; it is not part of creation (see the preceding and the following).

(12) The perfect "has come" (γεγονεν) indicates the new state of transgression (παραβασει) into which Eve entered (Knight, 144; Huther, 107). It is the consequence that follows in verse 15 (Mounce, 142), a permanent state (Robertson,

4:570). Interestingly, Paul does not say that it is "transgression" for women to teach men authoritatively, even though he uses "transgression" for what Eve did. Rather he says that he doesn't "permit" something to be done.

COMMENTS ON 1 TIMOTHY 2:15

(13) "She will be saved by the child bearing" is interpreted in various ways. It may refer (a) to physical salvation (White, 110; Huther, 108; Guthrie, 77–78; but Bernard, 49, and perhaps Robertson, 4:570, take it as both physical and spiritual); (b) to the joys and delights of Christian motherhood (Hendriksen, 111), or (best) (c) to spiritual salvation in the sense of a woman's (i) accepting her proper role in the church, or (ii) childbearing that is typical of the role of the woman of faith (Knight, 144–45; Mounce, 144; Robertson; Marshall, 470; etc.).

Knight (146 ff.) and others (Liefeld; Ellicott, 54; Lock, 33; Robertson, 4:570) take it that the childbearing refers to the birth of Messiah from Mary. To support this some (Oden and Liddon) appeal to the definite article involved: "the childbearing." Thus "she will be saved" refers first of all to Eve (she finds salvation in her distant seed, Jesus), then to any woman of faith of whom Eve is the type (it is not clear if this is the view of Mounce, 143–46). The future tense points to the future from the standpoint of the present era, or (with Knight, 147; Mounce, 143, Liefeld, 103) to the future from the standpoint of Eve.

(14) The preposition "through" ($\delta\iota\alpha$) (1 Timothy 2:15) is probably (a) instrumental, expressing means or agency: "she will be saved by means of the child bearing" (Knight; Oden, 102; Mounce, 147; Ellicott, 54; and most others), rather than (b) the idea of attendant circumstance, meaning that women are saved "in the experience of childbearing" (so White, 110). Yet, as another (c) view, Marshall (468) argues that the construction is somewhere between the first two options and is "loose and am-

biguous." He ends up deciding for circumstantial so as to avoid the charge that there may be grounds here for one's being saved "by" works (470).

(15) The condition, "if they remain in faith and love and holiness with self-restraint" (verse 15), points to the condition necessary for the Ephesian women to receive salvation and stay in it (Knight, 148). It has the force of a probable, future accomplishment (because of the presence of εαν). It involves faith and the necessary consequences accompanying faith. The "they" may point to (a) a shift from the singular woman/mother to all women, from the specific to the general; or to (b) the woman/wife and her husband (Quinn and Wacker, 233); or to (c) the woman and her children (Johnson, 202); or to (d) the children alone. The best is probably (a) (so Marshall, 471; Liefeld, 103; Barrett, 69: the singular is generic or a collective). The virtue of "self-control" is emphasized, and recalls verse 9: Women must be "chaste" (an emphasis found in the non-biblical literature above as the most important virtue of women).

SOME GENERAL OBSERVATIONS

Some concluding observations from interpreters of 1 Timothy 2 need to be mentioned. Mounce (148) makes an extended statement that the subordination or hierarchy that he finds in 1 Timothy 2 need not detract from the "essential equality" of men and women, that worth is not determined by role. The "equating of worth and role is a non-biblical, secular view of reality." Yet the assumption that 1 Timothy 2 is universal should itself be challenged. This is the focus of the next chapters.

Quinn and Wacker (240ff.) take the passage as a citation of an "already traditional parenetic charge" given to a bride at her marriage. Failure to recognize this, they observe, has lead commentators to suffer "acute, chronic theological dyspepsia about the demonstrative force of this citation . . . The citation does not and was never intended to prove anything." Yet they seem to offer no support for their claim.

Luke Timothy Johnson illustrates another way to deal with what some think is unacceptable to modern ears.[1] He simply does not approve of Paul's use of the Old Testament. He finds that Paul "defends male prerogatives and perspectives out of patriarchal reflex," when his sense of proper decency is threatened (206). His exegesis of Genesis needs to be corrected (208). Paul engages in a "faulty reading of Torah" (211). Thus Paul is not normative for the modern church, since, among other things, it is based "solely on Paul's individual authority" (211). Yet evangelicals cannot take such a dim view of Paul's writing. Why should this be said of Paul's teaching here and not also of other aspects of his teaching elsewhere? By what criterion, other than modern likes and dislikes, does one decide what is authoritative in Paul and what is not?

John Chrysostom (in *Discourse 4 on Genesis*) believed that in the original creation woman had a glory and an honor that was equal to man's. Yet (he wrote in *Discourse 2 on Genesis*) after the Fall, she was not equally God's image (defined not as essence but as authority), for she lost it and became subject to sin. Since the Fall "the female sex is weak and vain" and should not teach, unless her husband is an unbeliever (*Homily 9 on 1 Timothy*).[2]

It is especially helpful to read the comments of Marshall on this passage.[3] He believes that the passage is not universal teaching; it "is not absolute or for all time" (437–41). He evaluates the three major approaches. (1) It is a "universally binding prohibition of women teaching or holding any authoritative office in the church, since this would be incompatible with their subordinate position over against men." (2) The feminist position holds the same view of the text as (1) but then rejects the teaching by "a feminist hermeneutic." (3) The final view holds that the passage deals with a special church situation that "required unusual measures and/or that the teaching reflects a particular cultural situation and therefore should not be universalized" (438–39). Marshall rejects any literary relationship with 1 Corinthians 14:33–35. Instead both passages point to a tradition lying behind both and applied in different ways (439–40).

Finding that there was a false content to the teaching of some women that involved some form of "emancipatory tendency" that violated culture, Marshall (441) finds the author making three points: (1) He prohibits women teaching in a way that asserts authority over men (including their husbands); (2) he rejects their claim of superiority over men by affirming the order of creation and the event of Eve's deception; and (3) he affirms that childbearing, not teaching, is the accompaniment or means of salvation.

Marshall points out that the view that argues that the text is a universal prohibition does so on the basis of the appeal to the Genesis story, which is thought to "give a binding, scriptural principle" (442). The universal view also appeals to the need to correct tendencies toward greater emancipation that threaten the status quo. Marshall views the text as meeting the need to put "temporary restraints on freedom" flowing from "misconceived emancipation movements connected with false teaching" by women (443).

CONCLUSIONS

It seems to me that, all things considered, the passage should be understood as parallel with 1 Corinthians 11 and 14 and not to be interpreted in isolation from these. This suggests that culture is a serious consideration (since culture and custom are explicitly cited in 1 Corinthians 11 and 14).[4]

Liefeld (109) points to eight Biblical allusions in 1 Corinthians 11 to support women's wearing of head coverings, compared to two in 1 Timothy 2. Yet virtually everyone holds that 1 Corinthians 14 is not universal for today. This and other indications make it possible that 1 Timothy 2 is not universal and that the instruction is limited to a particular situation (a church-home) tied to Ephesus (note how Paul writes Corinthians from Ephesus, and Timothy is in Ephesus when Paul writes 1 Timothy to him). Paul saw some extreme tendencies at Ephesus and seeks to head off the same arising in Corinth before they go too far.

Less convincingly, Liddon (18) says that while 1 Corinthians 11 and 14 acknowledge that women at first did pray and prophesy, this was inconsistent with "women's natural position, and was withdrawn on this ground"—that is was "shameful" and was opposed by "the law" (1 Corinthians 14:35). He points out that in AD 308 the Council of Carthage forbade women to teach publicly (see also Ellicott, 52, and others).

At this point, I wish to commend the reader who has waded through all the finer points of the interpretation of 1 Timothy 2, as given above. I basically lean toward the view that does not see this text as universal.

Yet even if the exegesis of the elements of the text best supports its universality this universality need not stand forever. This is the point of the next chapters that treat the example of Sabbath observance and apply the paradigm of reality to the issue of the role of women in church ministry.

ENDNOTES

1. *The First and Second Letters to Timothy* in *The Anchor Bible* (New York: Doubleday, 2001).

2. Chrysostom is cited from Elizabeth A. Clark, *Women in the Early Church* (Wilmington: Michael Glazier, 1983), 34–35, 157–58.

3. I. Howard Marshall, *A Critical and Exegetical Commentary on the Pastoral Epistles* (Edinburgh: T & T Clark, 1999).

4. Merkle, "Paul's Arguments from Creation," 538–42 and notes 37–51, and most other complementarians see the situation at Ephesus and Corinth as very similar. Egalitarians tend to separate the situations in order to address the specific matter of women teaching and claim that it is restricted at Ephesus only because it was being abused there,

or otherwise a cause of concern, but the latter were not problems elsewhere and such teaching was common and allowable. Both the historical evidence and the contexts of the texts themselves support the similarity of the situations, including probably the matter of women teaching. However, in light of Paul's encouragement of prophecy, and his lifting this gift in various ways to the status of the best gift (see 1 Corinthians 12:28 and 14:1–39; Romans 12:6–8; Ephesians 4:11), it seems somewhat incongruous that women may prophesy and interpret prophecy (so 1 Corinthians 11 and 14) but not teach. Since "each one has a teaching" (1 Corinthians 14:26) it does seem that there were some differences between the situations, and this would be expected. Also, Paul says nothing in 1 Corinthians 11 or 14 regarding the deception of Eve (1 Timothy 2:14). Yet even on this point 2 Corinthians 11:3 warns the readers that Satan may corrupt them as he "deceived" (same word as in 1 Timothy 2:14) Eve. Paul does not say that women are more susceptible to this deceit.

5

The Significance of Paul's Appeal to Universals

THE PRIMARY question regarding the role of women that needs to be addressed concerns Paul's citation of universals in these texts to support the practices involved.[1] The crucial question is this: May an author cite a universal—defined here as something that is true and authoritative or normative for all time and for all places—to support a non-universal?

DOES AN APPEAL TO CREATION MAKE RESTRICTIONS ON WOMEN PERMANENT AND UNIVERSAL?

By this terminology, I purpose to distinguish some universals that are authoritative only for a limited time or place from those that are authoritative always for all places. An example of the latter is Christ's death as an atoning sacrifice. It is normative or authoritative for all times and places.

In 1 Timothy 2:12, Paul states that he does not permit a woman to teach in a "public and authoritative manner," nor to "exercise authority over" men.[2] In 1 Timothy 2:13, Paul appeals to the universal truth of the order of creation (Adam first, Eve second) and the dynamics of the Fall (Adam was not deceived but the woman was clearly deceived) to support his prohibition. In the similar non-permission in 1 Corinthians 14:34, Paul claims that what he writes is the "Lord's command" (verse 37).

Is Paul's statement, because he appeals to two universals, also universal and true for all time? Or is it historically limited and may be altered given different times and places (and circumstances)?

I think that it can be shown that an author's use of a universal to substantiate a particular practice does not make the particular practice a universal. Or, to put it differently, an author may cite a universal to support a non-universal—something historically and temporally limited.[3] While a practice may be universal (authoritative or normative) for some time and places, it need not be for all times and all places.

THE LESSON OF THE SABBATH

There seems to be a clear example of where a universal is cited to support a teaching and yet that teaching is no longer universal. I'm thinking here about the observance of the Sabbath day. In the giving of the Ten Commandments from Mt. Sinai, the fourth commandment (Exodus 20:8) reads, "Remember the Sabbath day by keeping it holy." The command is then substantiated by an appeal to a universal (20:11): "For in six days the Lord made the heavens and the earth, the sea, and all that is in them, but he rested on the seventh day. Therefore, the LORD blessed the Sabbath day and made it holy."

The institution of the Sabbath day rests on the universal of God's resting on the seventh day after creating for six days. Thus the observance of the Sabbath is substantiated by an appeal to a universal. We might make an initial conclusion that Sabbath observance is a universal.

At this point, I want to point out the parallel structure between this instance and the text of 1 Timothy 2:13: "For Adam was first formed, then Eve." The Greek of both texts at the point where they support the command begins with the connective "for" (γαρ), probably causal in both cases.[4]

Yet this is not the end of the matter. Most evangelicals disagree that Sabbath observance is a universal today, since the coming of Christ. How do we come to this conclusion?

There are several reasons. Most are located or signaled in the text of Scripture itself. When the Ten Commandments are repeated for the new generation about to enter Canaan, the reason given for observing the seventh day is changed. It is no longer an appeal to creation but the appeal to redemption. While the stipulations have not changed (Deuteronomy 5:12: "Observe the Sabbath day by keeping it holy, as the LORD your God has commanded you"; and verses 13–14 specify the particulars of the cultural obligation), the reference to the creation is dropped. Instead, there is the appeal to deliverance from Egypt: "Remember that you were slaves in Egypt and that the LORD your God brought you out of there with a mighty hand and an outstretched arm. Because of this [διὰ τοῦτο] the LORD your God has commanded you to observe the Sabbath day" (5:15).

Such a change occurs with none of the other commandments. While there is a slight addition added to the reason for observing the fifth commandment ("Honor your father and your mother"), the addition is very slight. The change regarding the fourth commandment is substantial: the former reason given in Exodus 20 no longer appears, and another appears. Indeed, the words do not specifically address or have a connection with Sabbath or seventh day observance. Instead, they are words tantamount to an expression of gratitude for what God has done. Yet such gratitude would be appropriate for observing all the commandments, not just this one.

The change in reason for observance of the command suggests a de-universalizing of the command. It is no longer universal for all (as the appeal to creation makes it the first time the command is given) but becomes in its second instance particular only for Israel. There is a progression of revelation, from a general universality or authority (for all peoples) to a particular or narrow universality or authority (for the second generation of Israel alone in light of its deliverance from Egypt). One could argue that the two differing reasons for observance are simply cumulative and to be added together, but in light of later revelation in the New Testament this is less likely.

In addition, none of the other commandments has such extended treatment in both places. No other one lists so many extenuating circumstances in which the Sabbath should be observed. Perhaps this suggests that no other commandment has such a direct bearing on daily (or weekly) life; no other needs to be so distinctly remembered.

All of this suggests that the fourth commandment is a heavy one, perhaps the heaviest of all as far as its impact on the ordinary life of a faithful Jew. It is also the commandment that represents a shift from the vertical dimension—paying proper honor to, and loving, God, his name and character—to the horizontal dimension—loving one's neighbor as oneself. It is the commandment that represents the hinge from one realm to the other: Paying honor to God by keeping one day a week holy is expressed in all kinds of relationships and responsibilities on earth.

Further attention to observance of the Sabbath day is continued by the prophets. Indeed, such observance is a key to whether the Jews are in obedience to God or not. It is a chief indication that in the age to come the Jews have become faithful to God, even during the new heavens and new earth! The references are Isaiah 1:13; 56:2, 4, 6; 58:13; 66:23; Jeremiah 17:21, 22, 24, 27 (twice in some of these verses); Ezekiel 20:12, 13, 16, 20, 21, 24, 22:8, 26; 23:38; 44:24; 45:17; 46:3, 4, 12—the last four in the context of the prince of the future. Interestingly, Sabbath-keeping is hardly mentioned in the twelve Minor Prophets. It occurs only in Hosea 2:11 and Amos 8:5.

Yet in spite of all of this evidence, it remains that Sabbath observance is not a universal. Jesus' statement that the Son of Man is Lord of the Sabbath (Matthew 12:18), and that the Sabbath was made for people, and not people for the Sabbath (Mark 2:27), paves the way for the non-observance of the Sabbath. He violated the Pharisee's scruples of Sabbath observance by healing on the Sabbath the man who had been blind from birth (John 9:16). The Pharisees, Jesus, and the people recognized that an issue of sin was at stake if Jesus truly violated the Sabbath by healing on it (9:16, 24, 25, 31, 34, 41). Related texts giving extensive treatment to the conflict over the Sabbath include Matthew 12:1–12; Mark 2–3; Luke 6, 13, 14; and John 5, 7, 9.

Then there is the witness of Paul the Apostle. Paul asserts that no believer should be judged on the basis of Sabbath observance (Colossians 2:16), for it is one of those things belonging to the shadow of the Old Testament, but the reality is found in Christ (verse 17) in the new covenant. Sabbath observance belongs to the old era. The implicit idea is that one should live on the level of the reality not the shadow. Observing one day as more sacred than another, or not observing such, is a matter about which everyone should be fully convinced in his own mind (see a similar discussion in Romans 14:5–6). In either case, the one who does observe the Sabbath and the one who does not observe the Sabbath "does so to the Lord" (verse 6).

It is clear, then, that Sabbath observance is not a universal that is authoritative or normative for today, in spite of all that the Old Testament might say. It is originally based in creation; yet this base does not in the end make Sabbath observance a universal. Some may observe it; most will not. Both are equally right before God and should be accepted before people, in keeping with Romans 14:1–15:13.

This understanding of Sabbath observance suggests a way to obviate the perceived universalism of the restrictions of Christian women in 1 Timothy 2:13–15, where Paul appeals to the universals of creation and the Fall. Paul may appeal to the proper covering for women who pray and prophesy (1 Corinthians 11), for their participation or non-participation in prophecy or speaking in tongues (1 Corinthians 14), and refuse to permit women to teach or exercise authority over men (1 Timothy 2:12), but none of these is a universal or normative for all times and places. They may violate tradition, avoidance of shame, and the proper cultural behavior of women (1 Timothy 2:9–11), but they are not sin or transgression, and are not universal. It is conceivable that with changing cultures and times, these things will take on a different form and/or become permissible.

This suggestion means that the meaning of 1 Timothy 2:13–14 (regarding the priority of Adam and the deceiving of Eve), while giving the cause for the instruction in verse 12, is not meant to universalize permanently the instruction in verse 12. The two verses rehearse historical information but represent the shadow not the reality. The reality is expressed in Galatians 3:28 and Colossians 2:17 and 3:11, in keeping with Genesis 1.

The appeal to creation is the *crux* of the issue—that the theological principle of headship, derived from creation, seems to be violated inherently by women teaching authoritatively or exercising authority over men. The biblical principle of submission is violated, since "the person who exercises authority over someone else is by definition in a position of authority with respect to that other person."[5]

There are at least three answers to this view: (1) Headship may not include submission (see the discussion on 1 Corinthians 11 above); (2) women are allowed to teach, prophesy, give revelation, etc. (in light of 1 Corinthians 11:2–16; 14:26ff.—none of the spiritual gifts are gender specific); and (3) even if it does include submission or subordination, the *actualizing of essential reality* in the new order "in Christ" (Galatians 3:28) may transcend the *order of creation* and the past order of what is appropriate *in the church and in culture* (the three frames of reference that Paul constantly has in mind). In Christ, there may be nothing improper for women (or wives) to be in a position of authority over men (or husbands), or vice-versa.

Yet how can Paul write the way he does? How can he write about subjection and even subordination on the one hand, and about equality on the other hand? What led him to affirm equality in Christ in the first place?

The answer, I believe, lies in a consideration of the worldview out of which Paul writes. This consideration leads to the next chapter.

ENDNOTES

1. Thomas R. Schreiner, "An Interpretation of 1 Timothy 2:9–15," in *Women in the Church: An Analysis and Application of 1 Timothy 2:9–15*, edited by Andreas J. Kostenberger and Thomas R. Schreiner (Grand Rapids: Baker Academic, 2005), 109, affirms as one of his chief points that the grounding of a prohibition in an appeal to creation indicates that the "command has universal validity." Yet this guideline does not apply to 1 Corinthians 11, apparently, where almost everyone acknowledges that wearing a covering in not a universal command, even though Paul cites the order of creation. Schreiner's is the same view as that of Merkle, "Paul's Arguments from Creation," 528. He says that the argument from creation "therefore is transcultural" (528). There is "no distinction between the underlying principle and the cultural expression of that principle" (542). For women to exercise authority over men violates the order of creation and repeats the failure of Eve that made her the leader of her relationship with Adam (543). Yet in Genesis 1 there is no division of labor or roles between Adam and Eve.

2. Schreiner, "Interpretation," 101–4, shows that this is plausibly what Paul meant. On the other hand, in parallel with the problems of 1 Corinthians 11 and 14, where much of the resolution rests on finding that wives and husbands meeting in homes with other wives and husbands were the cause of the problems, it may be that Paul's prohibition centers again on wives instructing husbands and exercising authority over them. Thus the prohibition parallels 1 Corinthians 14:34–35 where wives, not women in general (see notes above), are enjoined not to violate social decorum by embarrassing their husbands rather than respecting their special place as husbands, which is the wives' greatest virtue (as the

secular literature cited above shows). This explains why reference is made to the bearing of children in 2:15—only wives can do this.

The fact that Ephesus ties together all three texts (Paul wrote 1 Corinthians from Ephesus; and Timothy is at Ephesus) suggests that Paul saw violations of social decorum taking place at both, and moves to correct them.

3. Schreiner, "Interpretation," 110–11, takes up this kind of argument. He deals with 1 Timothy 4:1–5 and other passages and shows that such passages concern exceptions to the general pattern of equality at creation. Feminists illogically argue that creation is cited in 2:12–15 to support the exception—not permitting women to teach—while the rule is to allow them to teach.

My approach is different. I'm not saying that creation supports the exceptions. I'm saying that the appeal to the creation pattern does not make the prohibition necessarily universal (a crucial point that Schreiner argues, 105ff.), that there is support for the idea of equal roles in Genesis 1 where the role of male and female is presented as equal (to multiply and to rule the earth); and that the oneness of male and female in Christ has implications for roles. The parallel I'm citing relative to the Sabbath day shows that a creation norm may eventually be negated or surpassed in light of changing norms, culture, or revelation. Non-observance of the Sabbath is not simply an exception to observance; it has become the rule.

What I'm proposing in the parallel regarding men and women in ministry is that actualization of essential reality will mean that non-equality of roles should be the exception in light of additional revelation; equality of roles should be the rule when equality in Christ is actualized. Whether this is existential or historical reality now, or ever will be, is the crucial point.

Walter L. Liefeld, *1 and 2 Timothy, The NIV Application Commentary* (Grand Rapids: Zondervan, 1999), 106, approximates this concern relative to universals. He points to two complementary facts. (1) "Ethical practices and commands taught in Scripture are theologically grounded, even though they may apply to passing circumstances" (as examples he cites the instructions regarding the tabernacle in the wilderness, and Jesus' prohibiting verbiage in prayers); and (2) "the same theological truths that call for a particular response or set of practices in one circumstance may call for *different* responses and practices in other circumstances in order to be meaningful" (italics his; he cites the commands of Leviticus

19). (I would add also those commands of Leviticus 18 and 20). Liefeld (108ff.) also wisely cautions about the difficulty of assessing background data, the question of contemporary influences on interpretation (such as feminism), the specific singular use of a command in 2:11 (that a woman learn in submission), and the relevance of 1 Corinthians 11:2–16 for 1 Timothy 2 (a point I make below).

4. Schreiner, "Interpretation," 105–11, cites and refutes several arguments that attempt to diffuse the causal connection of verse 13 to the preceding verses.

5. Douglas Moo, "What Does It Mean Not to Teach or Have Authority Over Men?" in *Recovering Biblical Manhood and Womanhood*, edited by John Piper and Wayne Grudem (Wheaton: Crossway, 1991), 191.

6

Framing the Issue of the Role of Women in Church as a Matter of Worldview

THE RESOLUTION of the matter of the roles of women in ministry usually comes down to an egalitarian or a complementary position. On the whole, it seems that consideration of all the points of the exegesis of 1 Timothy 2 better supports the complementary position. This position is careful to make a difference between consideration of the roles of women versus the ontology or nature of women. This position holds that the roles are unaffected by or are consistent with the truth of the equality of men and women.

On the other hand, it is clear that two of the three categories ("slave nor free"; "Jew nor Greek") mentioned by Paul in Galatians 3:28 have changed their roles. This suggests that the third category ("male and female") may have changeable roles also.[1] Thus the larger context of Paul's teaching supports the egalitarian view.[2]

There may be a better way to deal with the role of women in ministry that balances the statements of Scripture. It is a position that goes beyond complementary and egalitarian terminology.[3] It is framed by recognition of the new order that Christ has inaugurated. It explicitly affirms a recognition of the difference that Christ has made.

CAN A NEW PARADIGM AID THE RESOLUTION OF THE QUESTION OF WOMEN IN CHURCH?

On other occasions, I've written about a paradigm of reality to express the Bible's worldview.[4] A worldview encompasses everything that exists, all that one thinks, and all that one does. The paradigm affirms two realms of reality and how one relates to the other.

In the Biblical worldview, there is existential or historically limited reality, which is physical, temporal, limited, and earthly. There is essential reality that is spiritual, eternal, unseen, heavenly—the realm of God and the spirit world. There is actualization: Essential reality is being actualized more and more fully in existential reality.

Every believer simultaneously exists in two realms—his/her historical, limited reality and his/her essential, spiritual reality. These two realms have existed ever since the creation of humanity and will endure throughout all the future. The tabernacle and temple of the Old Testament were visible reminders of the unseen, eternal realm existing among humanity. In the New Testament, because of their union with Christ, Christians are both citizens of earth (their existential reality) and of heaven (their essential reality).

The paradigm affirms both realms. The affirmation of both the physical and the spiritual prevents the errors of asceticism (withdrawing from the physical realm) and materialism (disavowing the spiritual realm). The third part of the paradigm, actualization, is crucial. By the power of the Spirit, the believer is to be actualizing the values and treasures of essential reality more and more in his/her daily experience.

I believe that this paradigm offers significant help in resolving the issue of the role of women in church. Yet to demonstrate its credibility for this issue, I need to show first how it is credible in understanding several other issues. In the next several pages, I seek to show how the paradigm is implicit to Scripture itself. It arises from the text.

THE PARADIGM IN SCRIPTURE

This paradigm with its three elements is reflected over and over in the Bible. Several passages reflect the paradigm especially well.

Second Corinthians 3:17–18 reads: "Now the Lord is the Spirit, and where the Spirit of the Lord is present, there is freedom. And we all, with unveiled faces reflecting the glory of the Lord, are being transformed into the same image from one degree of glory to another, which is from the Lord, who is the Spirit."

Freedom is essential reality. The words, "are being transformed" represent the actualizing of the essential reality of our identity in Christ into our daily experience—our existential reality. Second Corinthians 4:16–18 more clearly reflects this paradigm:

> Therefore, we do not lose heart, but even if our physical body is wearing away, our inner person is being renewed day by day. For our momentary, light suffering is producing for us an eternal weight of glory far beyond all comparison, because we are not looking at what can be seen but at what cannot be seen. For what can be seen is temporary, but what cannot be seen is eternal.

In this passage, the concepts of "our physical body," "light suffering," "what can be seen," and "temporary" represent our existential or historical reality and experience. The concepts of "our inner person," "eternal weight of glory far beyond all comparison," "what cannot be seen," and "eternal" represent our essential reality—our truest identity. And the actualizing of essential reality into our daily experience is reflected in the concepts of "is being renewed day by day," "is producing for us," and "we are looking at."

This third element is the key. There is a process under way by which Christians are being changed from what they once were naturally, in their unsaved state, to spiritual maturity so that they reflect more and more the character and person of Christ.

Virtually all agree that a biblical worldview encompasses the two realms of historical or existential reality and essential reality. Some call these the state and the standing of Christians. The words that one gives to these elements is unimportant. The important matter is that these concepts, these realities, exist and virtually all recognize them.

What is not readily recognized is the third element of the paradigm. There is a process that is already underway to actualize, to realize, more and more the essential or eternal realm in our existential, temporal realm. Notice that Paul in these two texts, and in many others, declares that such a process is already underway. The present tenses ("are being transformed" and "is being renewed day by day" and "is producing for us") draw attention to the process of implementation, of realization.

This expression of a biblical worldview pervades Scripture. Such an understanding is expressed in many other texts, such as Romans 12:1–2 and Colossians 3:1–4. Every exhortation in Scripture to change, to become more like Christ, is an exhortation to actualize, to realize, one's truest identity.

The paradigm is basic to all of Scripture. It reflects the worldview of the Bible. Even in the Garden of Eden it prevailed. Eve and Adam experienced actualization of the highest kind before the Fall. They dwelt in a physical realm in nakedness while simultaneously fully enjoying the reality of their experience of God. They were humans (historical reality) made in the image of God (essential reality). Eden was sort of heaven on earth. After the Fall, this balance of the two realities was severed, and essential reality was blocked, hindered, contaminated, and marred. Their nakedness became suddenly a matter of awareness and shame. It was not just a physical thing, for even after clothing themselves God addresses them (Genesis 3:11; see the present tense in the Greek translation, the LXX) as still naked: "Who told you that you are naked?" The clothing (existential reality) failed to hide their fall from innocence (essential reality).

APPLICATIONS OF THE PARADIGM TO VARIOUS INSTITUTIONS

The implications of such a paradigm are significant. It can be applied to matters of daily living, to theological positions, and to how one interprets the Scriptures.

The Home and Family

Applying the paradigm to the family means, for example, that my believing children, who are immature, are nonetheless my equals in Christ. Thus while this present era prevails children should always be in subordination, yet even so there should be an actualizing of their essential reality with their parents that affects how parents treat them and how they relate to their parents. Inherently such actualizing means, among other things, that parents, recognizing the essential reality of their children as "sons" or "daughters of God," cannot harshly treat their children, and that children cannot rebel against their parents.

Even children can see the implications of applying the paradigm to the family. On Mother's Day several years ago, I took my wife and our four children out for dinner at a modest restaurant. As we waited for our meal to be served, I shared with my family my thinking about the impact of this paradigm on our family. I had explained that the paradigm means that all of our children share with their parents an equal standing—an essential reality—before God as his sons or daughters fully accepted in Christ.

My youngest daughter, about ten years old at the time, immediately saw the implications. Reflecting on the fact that she was my equal in Christ, RuthAnn asked, "Dad, does this mean that you aren't going to spank us anymore?"

I answered, "No, it doesn't mean this, for I still fulfill the role of your father until you're grown, and will need to exercise discipline at various times. But it does mean that I have to respect you as a person, that I cannot treat you harshly, that I have to respect your being equal with me in Christ." She seemed to grasp the significance of what I said.

Every Christian belongs to a family by physical birth—his/her existential family, and to another family by spiritual birth—his/her essential family. All Christians realize at one time or another that appropriating the blessings of the body of Christ as family (actualizing essential reality) often brings the greater encouragement, help, and deliverance, and outweighs the horizontal level of belonging.

The State

Applying the paradigm to the Christian's responsibility to the state leads to the following. It is clear that every human being is a citizen of this world, that he owes allegiance to some earthly form of government, whether it be monarchial, despotic, and dictatorial, or democratic-republican in nature. Jesus clearly affirms some degree of allegiance to secular authority when he asserts that Caesar has authority over certain things pertinent to citizenship in a country (Matthew 22:15–22). This realm is the Christian's existential or temporal, day-to-day, reality or identity.

Yet according to Jesus (Matthew 22:15–22) there is another realm belonging to God to which the Christian gives allegiance, and this takes precedence over the other realm. Peter (1 Peter 2:13–17, "as free . . .") makes this clear when he affirms that the Christian is ultimately free of earthly citizenship; and Paul affirms the believer's heavenly citizenship (Philippians 3:20). In the truest or fullest sense of citizenship, Christians belong to no earthly state but fully belong to the heavenly one. This is essential reality.

What really matters in the end, should death at the hands of the secular state take place, is that one has citizenship in heaven. Actualizing the essential reality into the former existential reality leads to the great statements of not loving the world (1

John 2:15–17), of not being conformed to this world but being transformed according to a new pattern of thinking (Romans 12:1–2 and Colossians 3:1–4), of paying ultimate allegiance only to God and obeying Him, not men (so the apostles aver, Acts 5:29). Yet while Christians are the most free of all people, owing subservience to no earthly person or organization, they give up their freedom to become servants to all (1 Peter 2:16). Here actualization most clearly reflects the character of Christ.

The Workplace

The paradigm fits the workplace as well. Paul deals with those Christians who are servants or slaves of masters. While Christian slaves should obey their masters in every way (Colossians 3:22ff.), thereby acknowledging their historical or existential reality, they must do such subservience as ultimately to the Lord as their master and not to people (thereby acknowledging their essential reality). They serve the Lord Christ who will reward them (3:23–24). The actualizing of their essential reality means that they seek to please the Lord, serve sincerely and with enthusiasm (Colossians 3:22–23).

The institution of slavery or servitude was widespread in the Roman world of Paul. Many Christians were thus involved. But rather than exhort them to join the strikes or riots for freedom, which often occurred, Paul exhorts them to abide in their existential reality unless freedom was offered to them (1 Corinthians 7:21). Otherwise they are to reflect the character of Christ in being content with the situation in which they find themselves.

Human masters (an existential reality) are to treat—to actualize their essential reality—their slaves with justice and fairness (values belonging to essential reality), for they have a master in heaven (their essential reality).

The Church

The ultimately incongruous situation of having in any given local assembly both Christian masters and Christian slaves ultimately came to a head in AD 222. At that time, the first occurrence of a slave rising to the position of bishop of Rome showed the implications of Paul's statement that "in Christ there is neither slave nor free" (Galatians 3:28). Imagine the incongruity of the slave Callistus serving his master Monday through Saturday. He was totally subservient to him. But on Sunday, the master would listen to Callistus who would instruct him and the rest of the believers in the local church about the meaning of Scripture, including the meaning of Paul's instruction to slaves and masters. The master was to submit to the teaching of Callistus. The spiritual equality that slave and free had in Christ (essential reality) came to mean ultimately that the master had to set free his brother in Christ (the actualizing of essential reality in the historical setting). This is the assumption that Paul makes in the book of Philemon.

The role of shepherding the flock is the actualizing of essential reality in a given local assembly (an existential reality). Hence elders are to govern in ways modeled after Christ. Peter writes (1 Peter 5:1b–4):

> I urge the elders among you: Give a shepherd's care to God's flock among you, exercising oversight not merely as a duty but willingly under God's direction, not for shameful profit but eagerly. And do not lord it over those entrusted to you, but be examples to the flock. Then when the Chief Shepherd appears, you will receive the crown of glory that never fades away.

APPLICATION OF THE PARADIGM TO
THEOLOGICAL POSITIONS

It seems that the paradigm can be meaningfully applied to various theological positions. For example, one of the great questions related to eschatology concerns how the future will unfold. Will there be an actual, historical reign of Christ on the earth following His return that will go on for a thousand years (known as premillennialism)? Or is the future reign of Christ only figurative or spiritual, so that there is no physical reign for a thousand years (known as amillennialism)? It seems that the premillennial view stresses existential reality, and the amillennial view stresses essential reality. Viewed this way, it may be that both views are slightly skewed, over-emphasizing one feature over another. Thus the actualizing of essential reality (the third step in the paradigm) would lead one to consider that both views are correct in a sense, that the end will encompass a reign that is essentially spiritual, but this reign will be experienced on earth, since the way of God in the past is to embody essential reality in some sort of earthly "body." Prior to the New Testament, this actualizing on earth was expressed in the monarchy (Israel's king represented heaven's King) and in the tabernacle/temple.

Applying the paradigm to the resurrected body is helpful. Existentially there will be a resurrected spiritual "body" (essential reality) that has continuity with the present physical (existential) one. Yet actualizing the essential reality in the existential reality (the resurrection or transformation itself) means that the future body will be much more suited to the eternal realm (heavenly, not subject to decay and death, etc.) than the present, dying body is. Hence Paul describes death and the resurrection as the putting off of our "earthly dwelling" or tent and the putting on of our "heavenly dwelling . . . so that we might not be found naked" (2 Corinthians 5:1–10).

The paradigm may be applied to the future of the wicked, to those who die in a state of rejection of the gospel of Christ. Are they eternally in torment? Are they annihilated? The following resolution of the problem of the end of the wicked seems possible.

Believers, because of regeneration, experience essential reality and live on in the eternal realm. By virtue of their union with Christ they have immortality. Unbelievers, having rejected the person of Christ, never experience essential reality but are confined for eternity to existential reality—to a reality belonging to this realm of decay and death which is left behind in this age and universe and never participate in the great unfolding destiny of the righteous. This is how the unrighteous experience eternal death. They are not annihilated *per se*, but they continue to exist in a realm of temporal reality that never ends—a "second death" (Revelation 20).

APPLICATION OF THE PARADIGM TO HERMENEUTICS AND EXEGESIS: THE INTERPRETATION OF SCRIPTURE

The paradigm is particularly helpful for understanding prophecy and Scripture in general. For example, when God promises through the prophet Isaiah that a "virgin will conceive and bear a son, and you shall call him 'Emmanuel'" (Isaiah 7:14), the first level of meaning is the historical, grammatical sense. That is, there would be a child born to a young woman in the royal family whose birth and first years signaled divine intervention for King Ahaz and deliverance from the Assyrian invaders within a few years. This meaning of the text is the existential or historical level.

Yet beyond or beneath this level of meaning is the theological or essential meaning, which transcends the importance of the first level of meaning. This level of meaning points to the actual coming of the divine man born to a true virgin, and is cited appropriately at the birth of Jesus Christ to the virgin, Mary (Matthew

1:21). Jesus "will save his people from their sins." Matthew actualized the latent, deeper meaning by asserting that it was fulfilled in Christ.[5] Both meanings were in the text from the very first. The deeper meaning took many centuries before it was actualized.

The paradigm of the two realities can be applied meaningfully to the general pattern of prophetic Scripture. It is a significant contribution to answering the question: How is it that the New Testament (including Jesus and the apostles) often cites the Old Testament and finds meaning in ways that seem to be inconsistent with the widely accepted method of grammatical historical hermeneutics? The answer is that the method of the New Testament is not grammatical historical hermeneutics. It is something more. It includes the surface or grammatical meaning. Yet in light of the rest of the canon, the larger context, including worldview, the text includes something else. It is this something else which the paradigm of reality seeks to explain.

Just as there are two kinds of reality intersecting all the time for the Christian and his worldview, so there are two levels of meaning, which, while related and linked to one another, are embedded in the text and should be part of the Christians' hermeneutics. The meaning of any given text is not resolved until the possible essential and existential meanings have been sought. This means that the fullest meaning or interpretation of the Old Testament is not known until the possible additional meaning from the New Testament is added to it.

ALLEGORIES AND TYPES

This paradigm, then, encourages the search for types in the Old Testament, and even the existence of allegories, and explicates them. For example, regarding allegories, the paradigm explains why Paul, in his allegory (Galatians 4:21–31), can say that the Gentile and Jewish believers are the true offspring of Isaac and of promise, and that the Jews who can claim merely physical descent from Isaac but reject Christ are the offspring of Ishmael.

From a natural standpoint (existential reality), this interpretation is absurd and seems to violate Biblical history, and the Jews of Paul's day would reject it. But Paul is looking at the essential level of meaning in the Old Testament. What finally makes one a Jew is one's faith, not physical descent. One's physical identity is a mere accident of time (philosophically speaking), a historical matter. One's faith in Christ is what is essential or absolutely necessary to be called an heir of the promise to Isaac. It is this trait that determines one's truest identity, one's essential identity.

This is Paul's point in Romans 9:6–13. He writes that the seed of Abraham are not all his descendants, including those from both Isaac and Ishmael, or from both Jacob and Esau, but only those descendants traced from Isaac and his son Jacob. He concludes (9:8): "That is, it is not the children of the flesh who are children of God, but the children of the promise are regarded as descendants." "Flesh" pertains to the realm of historical or existential reality; "promise" pertains to the realm of essential reality, the realm that God fully rules.

This truth flows from within the Old Testament itself. While both Jacob and Esau could claim to be Jews, heirs of Isaac, only Jacob was, because he had faith in God's promise and Esau did not. Because Paul's contemporary Jews had rejected Christ they lost out on the promise fulfilled in Christ the seed of Isaac; but the Gentiles who accepted and believed in Christ became heirs of the promise given to Abraham and Isaac. Gentiles have to be linked to Christ as Abraham's seed to be heirs of the promise made to Abraham (Paul's point in Galatians 3:16, 22, 26–29). Paul concludes in verse 29, "And if you belong to Christ, then you are Abraham's seed, heirs according to promise." This verse comes just after the great statement of Galatians 3:28 that affirms the dissolution of distinctions because one is in Christ.

The pursuit of typology is an interesting and fruitful endeavor. A type is a person, institution or thing or event that has historically occurred and yet prophesies or points to a greater correspondence or counter to it later in Biblical history. The citing of Isaac as a type (in Hebrews 11:19) means that when God restored Isaac alive to Abraham instead of having him sacrificed Isaac prefigured the resurrection of Jesus Christ from the dead.

Typology is probably the number one method that early Christians used to discover the meaning of the Old Testament. Their authorization to engage in this practice came from Jesus Himself, who both by his example (cf. John 3:13–14, and many other examples) and by His instruction, encouraged Christians to read Scripture this way. His instruction calls for His followers to discover Him throughout the Old Testament, and this surely includes typology (a form of indirect prophecy) as well as direct prophecy. He said to confused followers after His resurrection (Luke 24:25–27, 44–45):

> "O foolish men and slow of heart to believe in all that the prophets have spoken! Was it not necessary for the Christ to suffer these things and to enter into his glory?" And beginning with Moses and with all the prophets, he explained to them the things concerning himself in all the Scriptures ... "These are my words which I spoke to you while I was still with you, that all things which are written about me in the Law of Moses and the Prophets and the Psalms must be fulfilled." Then he opened their minds to understand the Scriptures.

To read the Bible Christologically is the call to every Christian.

Paul reinforces this approach to reading Scripture. Not only does he find types (Romans 5:12 and 1 Corinthians 9:8–10), but he says that such typology was written for Christians' instructions. He says that all the events that occurred for Israel in their Exodus from Egypt were typical for Christians (1 Corinthians 10:5, 11): "Now these things happened as types for us, that we should not crave evil things, as they also craved; ... Now these things happened to them as a type, and they were written for our instruction, upon whom the ends of the ages have come."

Do we catch how significant Paul's words are? What Paul is saying is that from the very beginning, at the inscripturation of the Old Testament, it was part of the divine Author's intention to include a depth of meaning intended for those living after the coming of Christ. Thus the meaning of the Old Testament is not fully explained within its own context, but the New Testament is part of the context for determining the meaning of the Old Testament.

Indeed, the future significance or meaning for New Testament people became part and parcel of the original enunciation of promise in the Old Testament. Referring to Genesis 12:1–3, Paul writes in Galatians 3:8, "And the Scripture [here personified, and used in place of "God"], foreseeing that God would justify the Gentiles by faith, preached the gospel beforehand to Abraham, saying, 'All the nations shall be blessed in you.'" The fact that the gospel proclaiming justification by faith would be preached after the coming of Christ to the Gentiles affected how God spoke the promise to Abraham, what words he used, millennia before Christ came.

In summary, the Old and New Testaments are full of types, and Christians should read their Bible eagerly expecting to discover more than even what the inspired writers of Scripture discovered. This is so because the worldview of what reality consists affects the very wording of the text.

THE MEANING OF PROMISE

Such an understanding goes to the heart of the meaning of promise as enunciated initially to Abraham (Genesis 12:1–3). God promises Abraham a land and a great nation or seed (descendants) through whom all the nations would be blessed. Existentially or historically, this promise was encapsulated in the covenant that God made with Abraham as described in Genesis 17. On the historical or existential level the Abrahamic Covenant promised to Abraham the land of Canaan (15:7, 13, 18) and physical posterity or descendants (15:4–6, 13–21).

Yet another level meaning was also involved from the very beginning, reflecting a Biblical worldview of reality. Behind or alongside the physical reality of a land and seed there was also a spiritual or unseen or eternal reality of a land and seed. The latter are clearly understood from the book of Hebrews in the New Testament. Corresponding to the land of Canaan the New Testament author says that Abraham and his heirs were actually searching for a heavenly country (Hebrews 11:13–16) and an eternal seed (namely Christ) of whom Isaac is a type by virtue of his rescue from being sacrificed (11:19). It is well worth quoting these verses:

> All these [Abraham, Sarah, and their descendants who lived by faith] died in faith, without receiving the promises, but having seen them and having welcomed them from a distance, and having confessed that they were strangers and exiles on the earth. For those who say such things make it clear that they are seeking a country of their own. And indeed if they had been thinking of that country from which they went out, they would have had opportunity to return. But as it is, they desire a better country, that is a heavenly one. Therefore God is not ashamed to be called their God; for He has prepared a city for them.

Thus the Biblical worldview of reality and meaning involves always these two elements—what is historical and what is eternal. Therefore, it is clear that Christians today, following the pattern laid down in the Old Testament, seek a heavenly land and a "heavenly" seed. Hebrews 12:22–24 affirms that Christians of any generation "have already come to Mount Zion and to the city of the living God, the heavenly Jerusalem . . . and to Jesus, the mediator of a new covenant, and to the sprinkled blood, which speaks better things than the blood of Abel."

The author affirms once more that believers seek another realm, a heavenly (essential) one, while they live on earth (their existential realm) (13:14). "For here we do not have a lasting city but we are seeking the city which is to come." All these statements affirm that the worldview of Christians is the same as that of the Old Testament saints.

THE BIBLICAL WORLDVIEW AS EXPRESSED IN THE BOOK OF HEBREWS

Actually, the whole book of Hebrews has as its understanding of reality this distinction between the existential and the essential. His treatment of Melchizedek (7:1ff.) follows the pattern of discovering beyond the physical meaning of who he is (verses 1–2) a spiritual meaning, so that he is "without father, without mother, without genealogy, having neither beginning of days nor end of life, but made like the Son of God, he abides a priest perpetually." It is the divine Author of Scripture who has made him like the Son of God.

It is necessary to cite only a few verses from chapters 8–10 that highlight this worldview that distinguishes between the realms of the physical or temporary and the spiritual or eternal. Hebrews 8:2 identifies Jesus as a "a minister in the sanctuary, and in the true tabernacle, which the Lord pitched, not man." The priests on earth are identified (8:5–6) as those:

> . . . who serve as a copy and shadow of the heavenly things, just as Moses was warned by God when he was about to erect the tabernacle; for, "See," he says, "that you make all things according to the pattern which was shown you on the mountain." But now he has obtained a more excellent ministry, by as much as he is also the mediator of a better covenant, which has been enacted on better promises.

In his central passage (Hebrews 9:11–12), the author goes on to distinguish two levels of reality:

> But when Christ appeared as a high priest of the good things to come, he entered through the greater and more perfect tabernacle, not made with hands, that is to say, not of this creation; and not through the blood of goats and calves, but through his own blood, he entered the holy place once for all, and obtained eternal redemption.

Again, the author distinguishes the two realms of heaven and earth when he writes,

> Therefore it was necessary for the copies of the things in the heavens to be cleansed with these, but the heavenly things themselves with better sacrifices than these. For Christ did not enter a holy place made with hands, a mere copy of the true one, but into heaven itself, now to appear in the presence of God for us (Hebrews 9:23).

Here the things on earth are merely "copies" of the truer reality of heavenly things.

Finally, the author pictures the law and all that belongs to it, as a shadow of a greater reality realized or actualized in Christ. He writes, "For the law, since it has only a shadow of the good things to come and not the very form of things, can never by the same sacrifices year by year, which they offer continually, make perfect those who draw near" (Hebrews 10:1).

This terminology is similar to Paul's sweeping statement, that various practices of drinking and eating and observing holy days "are merely a shadow of what is to come, but the body [or reality or substance] belongs to Christ" (Colossians 2:17).

APPLICATION OF THE PARADIGM TO THE ROLE OF WOMEN IN MINISTRY

Now all the preceding texts are meant to show how deeply embedded in the text and the interpretation of Scripture the paradigm of reality truly is. It is a pervasive, all encompassing approach to interpretation and to the solving of challenging texts. It acts as a grid through which to see or understand the total meaning of Scripture.

I finally come to the role of women in church. If the application of the paradigm works to explaining a myriad of texts it should help to solve the question of the role of women in ministry. And it does.

The application of this paradigm to the role of women in ministry may be summarized as the following: The limitations of women in ministry expressed in the three texts discussed in the above chapters comprise existential reality. They are to keep their heads covered when praying or prophesying (1 Corinthians 11); they should not speak out of place when the church gathers in a home (1 Corinthians 14); they should not teach men in an authoritative manner, thus fulfilling the role of elders (1 Timothy 2).

The equality of women with men in their being, in their nature, because they are equal in Christ (Galatians 3:28 and Colossians 3:11), is essential reality. It is anchored in their spiritual identity.

Day by day, the equality of women with men in various aspects is to be actualized in roles more and more. This is the pattern as it should be and will be. Actualization is the third element of the paradigm.

The essential equality of the roles of men and women is anchored in Genesis 1 where both males and females bearing the image of God are given the charge to multiply and to rule the world. Genesis 2 adds to Adam's roles that of his naming of the animals and his naming of Eve. Genesis 3 reveals that the woman will bear children, that her desire will be to dominate him, that he will rule over her, and that the male will farm and toil under adverse circumstances. The role of bearing children will "save women," Paul says (1 Timothy 2:15). It signals that she is keeping true to her role from Genesis 1–3. Childbearing, along with perseverance in faith, love, holiness, with self-control, are the necessary consequences of a woman's saving faith.[6]

The role of bearing children is a role that women will do for the course of this age, but will cease in the era to come. It is part of the physical, unchangeable nature of women. Yet even this role is not essential to the identity of women—that a female be a mother.

The role of women being teachers of men or exercising authority over men—doing the work of an elder—seems also to accord with Genesis 1–3. It seems that both men and women may fulfill this role. This role for women does not seem barred by the physical way that the woman was made.

While child-bearing is limited to women because of their physical makeup, which will not change during the course of the present age, it is difficult to see how teaching men is somehow to be denied to women because of their physical makeup. Teaching men is not a matter necessarily restricted to men because of physical makeup. Nor is it, in light of the paradigm of reality, a matter of essential reality. It is an existential reality. Whether men or women should engage in teaching men comes down finally to the essential reality or identity of men and women. And there is nothing in essential reality—in their essential identity—that should bar women from teaching and/or exercising authority over men.

REVERSAL CHARACTERIZES THE NEW ERA IN CHRIST

Reversal is a key concept of the new era in Christ. What has been the pattern or process in the past, under the old era of the law, has been altered and reversed in many ways. For example, God has now elevated Gentiles who place faith in Christ to the position of the children of Isaac in place of the natural children of Isaac who do not believe in Christ (see Galatians 4:28–31). Reversal has implications for the customary roles of men and women who have become Christians.

Since the essential identity of believers as "one in Christ Jesus" has been quite well actualized in the *roles* that "slaves and free" and "Jew and Greek" (Galatians 3:28) have today in most cultures, it should be expected that the essential identity of "male and female" should also be actualized more and more in their *roles* in contemporary culture. Some actualization, it seems, must take place this side of eternity. Given enough time and enough changes in culture such will occur. In the eternal era it seems that there will be no distinctive roles for men and women.

I recognize that the categories of Galatians 3:28 are not equal or of the same kind, since "male . . . female" goes back to creation and the other two do not, as pointed out by other writers.[7] Yet it seems that "one in Christ" should have implications for the totality of all of living, including roles for males and females in society and in the church in particular. The paradigm of reality is a way to actualize this truth.

So how do we decide if other statements are universals when they parallel the kind of things that Paul does here? As for so many other questions, the key is context—the context of the rest of the teaching of Jesus and Paul, and the context of culture.

A serious concern usually arises at this point. How does one avoid compromising moral or ethical standards? How does one recognize what part of the law is no longer valid? How does one distinguish what is permanently wrong morally and what is an amoral practice?

If something in the culture violates or contradicts, for example, one of the Ten Commandments or its extrapolation, then it is wrong. Culture cannot abrogate or transgress the nature of God or what has been revealed in the teaching of Christ.

We must make a distinction between matters that truly involve essential reality and the immorality that violates it, and those that do not. There is nothing in the context that identifies authoritative teaching by women as a matter of morality, nor anything in the context that compromises what male and female are essentially if a female engages in teaching. I address this matter further in the next chapter.

Another view of this entire discussion suggests that the text teaches the subordination of women, but that the forms of that subordination may change.[8] While the form of fulfilling a command may differ—women wearing a veil when praying or prophesying, or women being prohibited from teaching men—the content stays the same: women should show submission to men, or at least give deference to them. Perhaps this submission today takes the form of wearing a wedding ring or something else. This is a more moderate position.

Yet this position fails to recognize that essential reality (being one in Christ) is to be progressively actualized/contextualized now that Christ has come. It is progressively being realized, since during the course of time custom or culture changes, the church grows in maturity, and the implications of the truth of the gospel become more and more realized in the institutions of a culture/society. Thus some practices change or start or stop during the course of time. What was perhaps forbidden in the past becomes allowable in the present or future.

CONCLUSION

The paradigm outlined above is a different way to address the question of the role of women in church. It is a more Biblical way to resolve the issue than the way of the complementary and egalitarian views.

The above discussion of the paradigm affirms the essential equality of women and men and how the actualization of the paradigm of reality finds that women may engage in virtually any role that men have in society and in church. Yet the paradigm calls for a recognition of existential reality also. Existential reality also must be satisfied or accommodated. Culture and history are existential reality. Hence while women by essential reality are free to do what men do, the existential reality of culture may not permit this.

It seems that the limitations of existential reality are yet operative in a significant way in most cultures today. Thus women in America and elsewhere are probably not free to do everything that men do in church. In the next chapter, I discuss when and how such limitations may cease.

ENDNOTES

1. Perhaps the allowance of women authoritatively teaching men has a parallel with what happened with slaves and masters. From AD 217 to 222, Callistus, a slave, held the position of bishop of Rome (see H.P. Liddon, *Explanatory Analysis of St. Paul's First Epistle to Timothy* [rep. Minneapolis: Klock and Klock, 1978, 72]). Christianity brought about a change in culture regarding slavery. In a similar manner, Christianity is bringing about a change in culture regarding the status of women. No other belief system or religion has done either of these. It seems that, in certain settings (on the mission field, and often in the third world), women already teach men authoritatively, including the proper roles of men and women (because they are better gifted to do so; or because the only men available are immature believers).

2. Liefeld, *Timothy*, 113–14, identifies this same contrast. The strength of the complementary view is its focus on the words and grammar of the text, but its neglect of wider contexts. On the other hand, the strength of the egalitarian view is its focus on the specific circumstances of the letter, but the danger is in distorting the background materials. Thus Liefeld chooses a third alternative that brings together the exegetical elements and the context. Paul did not choose to put his instruction into imperatives for all times and places, but the teaching is not limited to the conditions of Ephesus but apply to the whole ancient culture. In keeping with the fact that Paul's missionary purpose was foremost, we should facilitate that same purpose in our social context "rather than repeat the same restrictions that were appropriate then but can be a hindrance to conversions now" (114). Liefeld, 110–14, also encourages the church today to see the spiritual benefits of having proper attitudes, to see how theology, morality, and custom relate, to be consistent, and to ask the right questions to determine whether a text is universal or

not. Prayer, holiness, modesty, and the virtues of 1 Timothy 2:15 need to be pursued today.

3. Liefeld, *Timothy*, 105, warns about the limitations of such labels. He prefers calling the positions, "restrictive" and "unrestrictive." This is a wise suggestion.

4. For example, in James B. De Young and Sarah L. Hurty, *Beyond the Obvious* (Gresham: Vision House; 1995).

5. See my co-authored *Beyond the Obvious*, which seeks to apply the paradigm of reality to the pursuit of hermeneutics. It is subtitled: *Discover the Deeper Meaning of Scripture*. Others have drawn attention to this way of reading Scripture. For example, Darrell Bock calls these two levels of meaning the "historical-exegetical" reading and the "theological-canonical" reading of the text. See his "Use of the Old Testament in the New," in *Foundations for Biblical Interpretation*, edited by David S. Dockery, *et al* (Nashville: Broadman & Holman, 1994), 97–114. The terminology of "existential" and "essential" is better than that of "exegetical" and "theological" because it is broader and can apply across all pursuits of learning and experience. It is not just limited to hermeneutics. It expresses a worldview and everything comes within a worldview, including what is real, what is true or truth, and what is moral or ethical. All that one can think about or do is determined by one's worldview.

6. So Schreiner, "Interpretation," 118–20, interprets verse 15.

7. See his "Role Distinctions in the Church," in *Recovering Biblical Manhood and Womanhood* (Wheaton: Crossway, 1991), 160–63.

8. See Grant R. Osborne, *The Hermeneutical Spiral* (Downers Grove: InterVarsity, 1991), 318–38.

7

Summary and Conclusions

What Does the Future Horizon Look Like?

IN THE following pages, I wish to summarize the preceding discussion and draw out several conclusions from our study of 1 Corinthians 11 and 14, and 1 Timothy 2. I will suggest a final resolution of this study that is somewhat surprising.

We began this study by asking whether or not women may engage in the same things that men do in the local church. The primary focus of this and all such discussions is whether women may teach men and/or exercise authority over them. Women in America (and the West in general) engage in the same activities and practices that men do in virtually all pursuits and institutions of society. It is only in the local church that the question still arises: Are evangelical women barred from certain practices?

The traditional approach (what is known as the complementary view) takes the view that women may not teach and/ or exercise authority over men in the local assembly of believers. They should not be seen as fulfilling the role of elders who instruct authoritatively the rest of the church.

The more recent view (although it has ancient antecedents) that is challenging the traditional view is usually called the egalitarian view. This view asserts that men and women in Christ are equal and are not to be barred from doing anything in the church, including the authoritative instruction of the rest of the church. This view is usually based on a nuanced interpretation of the central texts.

Here I wish to enumerate the points covered in the book. These points are cited with brevity and succinctness.

1. On the basis of the creation, but especially the Fall, there is an order derived from Genesis that suggests the pre-eminence of men. This is parallel to the relationship of God and Christ. Yet women are not inferior to men, nor are they essentially subordinate to men. In certain cultures they may have to be submissive to men but they are not subordinate to them. In a sense it can be said that men and women, male and female, are equal in Christ, but husbands and wives are not. This statement anticipates the significance of a new paradigm as applied to the role of women in ministry.

2. Paul's chief concern is that Christians, privately or in public worship, should not violate cultural norms so as to bring unnecessary slander to the gospel.[1] The concern of believers is to exalt Christ, who made Himself servant to all. Their concern is not to exalt their freedom.

3. In all three of these passages, Paul does not label the violation of the "traditions" as "sin" or "trespass" or any such term. Violation is not a moral issue or a matter of sin but an issue of "shame" or "impropriety" (11:4–6, 13–14), "the nature of things" (11:14), "custom" (11:16), and "disorder" or disruption (14:33, 40).[2] Disregarding what Paul has written is not even said to be a "violation" *per se* of creation or the "law."

4. I have introduced into the discussion of the roles of men and women in the local church the matter of a biblical worldview. It is my contention that the larger context of these passages must be considered in the interpretation of the separate texts. The larger context concerns the matter of worldview—what the Bible teaches about the nature of reality, truth, and ethics.

5. I've advocated a particular paradigm to explain the biblical worldview as expressed in such places as 2 Corinthians 3:18 and 4:16–18. It consists of three elements: existential or his-

torical reality, essential reality, and actualizing of the latter into the former. Existential reality concerns that which is changeable, temporary, limited, earthly, and historically limited. Culture goes here, as do the roles of men and women in the local church.

Essential reality concerns what is unchangeable, eternal, unlimited, heavenly, and transcending history. The believer's standing or reality or equality in Christ goes here, as do such concepts as freedom, forgiveness, the fruit of the Spirit, the resurrection body, the realities of heaven, and more.

The third element of the paradigm is actualization. This means that there is ongoing and growing actualizing or realizing of one's equality in Christ in daily living. More and more the Christian is to become more and more holy. More and more one's existential reality should reflect and assume the effects of essential reality.

6. The two considerations based on the order of creation or the Fall and culture must be balanced by actualizing the transformation that Christ introduced. The essential reality of men and women in Christ is that they are one, hence equal in essence. Texts such as Galatians 3:28 and Colossians 3:10–11 affirm essential equality in Christ. Both men and women in Christ are being conformed, and renewed, more and more "in knowledge after the image of God who created the new person in Christ, where there is neither Greek nor Jew, circumcised or uncircumcised . . . but Christ is all and in all" (Colossians 3:10–11; compare 1 Corinthians 12:13). Our goal on earth should be to actualize by the Spirit as much of this equality as possible. Certainly we are not to wait till heaven for this to be realized.[3]

Many statements in the texts under consideration point to the overriding matter of identity in Christ: "nevertheless, in the Lord" (1 Corinthians 11:11), "but everything comes from God" (11:12); "as to the Lord" (Ephesians 5:22); "as it is fitting in the Lord" (Colossians 3:18; cf. similar expressions in verses 17, 20, 22, 23, and 4:1); "as is proper for women who profess reverence for God" (1 Timothy 2:10); and others. Where identity in Christ is not in a given passage, it is always in the larger context and should be part of the interpretation of any passage.

7. The foregoing from Paul finds its basis in the example and teaching of Jesus, who was very progressive for His day regarding the role and place of women. By both His example and instruction, Paul emulated Jesus.

8. The basic principle is that Christians give up their freedom in Christ in order to serve others, and to avoid unnecessary slander or opposition to Christian witness and ministry, which attends the violation of local norms or customs. This is the principle embedded in these texts, and frequently affirmed in Scripture (note Romans 14:1–15:13; 1 Corinthians 7–11; especially Galatians 5:1–13; 1 Peter 2:13–16; etc.). Paul could become all things to all people in order to save some (1 Corinthians 9:19–26).

Perhaps there is an internal indication reflected in the history of the texts that witnesses to the difficulty of actualizing correctly the paradigm of essential reality. Paul wrote Galatians 3:28 around AD 47–49 in what is probably his earliest epistle. When he later repeats the essence of the verse (in Colossians 3:11), he leaves out the third pair of "male and female." This was written about AD 63.

Could it be that, after the initial writing, Paul observed that the churches he founded or influenced misunderstood what he was saying and tried to actualize the essence of this category too far? Hence he is led to correct misunderstanding when he pens 1 Corinthians (about AD 55–56), and leaves out mention of the third group when he writes Colossians, and leaves out the whole idea when he writes 1 Timothy (about AD 64–65). This consideration, however, does not suggest that the particular abuses of the paradigm should abrogate the paradigm and its actualization in other ways, times, and places.

HERMENEUTICAL (INTERPRETIVE) CONCERNS

In conclusion, all three texts (1 Corinthians 11; 1 Corinthians 14; 1 Timothy 2) are basically parallel. All speak of cultural matters, not of transcultural or universal matters. All may actually concern the relationship of husbands and wives, not men and women in general. All of the texts support the cultural matters by appeals to universals (the creation, the Fall). Yet such an appeal does not make the behavior universal, as the parallel with the non-observance of the Sabbath in the New Testament shows.

In the case of 1 Corinthians 14, the appeal is to "the law." If this is really an appeal to culture, as I argue above, then this suggests that the other two appeals to universals amount to the same thing—using a universal to support a social convention. In the case of 1 Timothy 2, we should simply do what Paul does in 1 Corinthians 11:11–12—qualify his instruction with "in the Lord."

What is truly universal is the universality of differing customs. With their hearts always set on equality in Christ, Christians give up their "rights" and allow local culture to determine finally how they do ministry.

Two hermeneutical principles are present: relate the meaning of a text to the overarching concerns about actualizing essential reality; and the Spirit continues to teach the Church how both form and content may change.[4] One's hermeneutic is not static. Rather, one employs a hermeneutic derived from the New Testament's use of the Old Testament. Such a hermeneutic finds richer meaning in the text—it actualizes the essential or deeper, Christological meaning behind the literal, historically limited (existential) meaning. This hermeneutic is justified since it reflects a biblical worldview of reality (as defined above) and follows New Testament precedent.

There is a parallel between reading the Old Testament Christologically and reading the New Testament Christologically—

what it means to be "in Christ." The former points to what has later been realized (actualized) in the era of Christ.

CONCLUSION: THE FUTURE HORIZON

All of Paul's teaching regarding the role of women in ministry is culturally limited. Yet this does not mean that it can be disregarded. It means that the role of women may differ from culture to culture.

It means that, for the foreseeable future, women will not have roles equal to men in every respect. During this era, gender differences exist, and only women bear children. Marriage is a fixture of this era. These disappear only in the future era when humans will be like angels, when they no longer marry nor parent children (1 Corinthians 7:1, 13:1; Luke 20:35).

Many believe that the problems at Ephesus and Corinth can be traced to an "over-realized eschatology"—that the Christian women believed that the era of transformation, the kingdom, had already arrived. The believers believed that the rubric, "already but not yet," was to be understood as, "already even now!"

We can draw out this distortion in another direction as well. At present it is those of the complementary view who fault egalitarians as following an "over-realized eschatology." Yet it seems that those of the complementary view are caught up in an "under-realized" eschatology. They believe that the rubric is, "not now nor ever."

THE PARALLEL WITH SLAVERY

The case of slavery is a good parallel to the matter of women in church. In the New Testament there is a tacit acknowledgement of slavery as a cultural phenomenon. Paul's instruction is to continue in the state in which one is found when one becomes a Christian. Hence Paul's instruction is, in general, for slaves to be good slaves and masters to be good masters—seeking to please God rather than people (consider Colossians 3:22–4:1). Yet in one place Paul encourages slaves to pursue freedom if they are offered such (1 Corinthians 7:21). Slaves are to actualize their essential equality in Christ (Galatians 3:28 and Colossians 3:11) if the culture permits.

Subsequent history illustrates how equality in Christ could not long omit the liberation of slaves in the church, and subsequently in society. In the year AD 222, for the first time a slave rose to the position of the bishop of the church in Rome. We cited this illustration above.

The conflicted situation where culture affirmed inequality in domestic affairs but the Bible via Paul affirmed equality in Christ could not last forever. In due time, Christians opposed slavery within the church and without—using their influence to change state institutions. While this conflict eventuated in the Civil War in the United States, it was a conflict that had to be resolved, and resolved in only one direction.

It remains for some countries, Islamic countries, to come to the same position on slavery as the rest of the world. Yet Islamic countries have no Biblical mandate, such as equality in Christ, to come to the abolition of slavery, for Islam rejects the epistles of Paul as authoritative for it. Should Islam come to a total renunciation of slavery, it will be the result of the impact of Christian values, not Islamic values, on various countries.

A PRINCIPLE OFFERING HOPE
AS NEVER BEFORE

As never before, the question of the role of women in church has, indeed, special implications for contemporary times. On the one hand, there is today a greater restraint on change or actualization of equality than in Paul's day. In light of modern, instant communication and globalization, Paul's reminder not to violate culture (i.e., "you maintain the traditions as I delivered them to you" [1 Corinthians 11:2]; "we have no such custom, nor do the churches of God" [11:16]; and "as in all the churches of the saints" [14:33]) takes on a scope far greater and weightier than Paul ever knew. The contemporary church at any particular place is called to be sensitive to a truly global church. Virtually instant communication makes it possible for churches everywhere else to know what a given local church may be doing. Such a concern could never have been so deeply important in any period of the church before the present. These are historic times.

On the other hand, this globalization means that there is unprecedented opportunity to actualize essential reality more quickly and more pervasively. There should be progressively growing equality of women with men in ministry, as culture allows, as the church continues to mature and grow around the world. Through mutual interchange the church worldwide can benefit from instruction arising from any given local church. This situation has never before been known in the history of the church. These are *truly* historic times.

The increased speed of communication and its implications point to a principle: *The sooner and wider the giving up of freedom occurs, the sooner and wider the realization of freedom follows.*

Christians are the most free of all people (consider 1 Peter 2:16). Yet they use their freedom to forego it and to give it up. Instead, they restrict and submit themselves to others. In so doing they ensure that freedom will follow more quickly and pervasively. The church is growing both numerically and in maturity. The church is further along in becoming fully mature than it has ever been before. Both Scripture (Matthew 11:12 and 16:18–19; Colossians 1:6, 28–29 and 2:19; Hebrews 11:39–40; etc.) and experience support this. And this growing maturity will take on exponential growth because of increasing global communication and interaction.

So if we end up affirming that, at present, women in the church should not teach authoritatively nor exercise authority over men, what is the difference from the standard complementary position? Just this: that Christians should recognize that this limitation is cultural, not a universal; that it will be dispensed with in time as equality in Christ is fully actualized.

The application of the paradigm of reality also means that both positions, the egalitarian and the complementary, are partially correct, yet they are shortsighted and incomplete, and therefore faulty.[5] It is time to stop forcing the discussion into one side or the other. There is a viable option to both.

SOME CRUCIAL AND PRACTICAL MATTERS

Many people express concerns about where the position advocated in this study may lead. Most of these are probably red herrings or baseless, but need to be addressed. I deal with them under the following questions.

Some are concerned about the growing oneness expressed in the roles that males and females may experience. (1) Does the growing liberation of women not parallel the issue of homosexuality—that the Church should grow in its tolerance and affirmation of homosexual behavior? Yarbrough raises this issue as one of several reasons to reject an egalitarian view of men and women.[6]

The answer is an emphatic "no" for the following reasons. (a) Homosexuality, in both testaments, is clearly labeled "dishonorable passions," "against nature," "shameless acts," "a due penalty for error" (Romans 1:26–27), as an example of "ungodliness and unrighteousness," "suppressing the truth by their unrighteousness," "exchanging the glory of the immortal God for an image" of idolatry, not "glorifying God," etc. (Romans 1:18–23). It is also described as something that prevents one from "inheriting the kingdom of God," as belonging to the past of those who are now "washed," "sanctified," and "justified" (1 Corinthians 6:9–11). It is something to be proscribed by law, given to curb the behavior of the "lawless and rebellious, the ungodly and sinners, the unholy and profane" (1 Timothy 1:8–10). (b) Homosexual behavior is viewed as violating natural moral law—both within and outside of Scripture (consider Aristotle, Plato, etc.). (c) Scripture assigns criminal penalties for homosexual behavior (Leviticus 18:23 and 20:13). None of these matters characterizes the change of the traditions regarding women—toward the equality of women. (d) Homosexuality is prideful rebellion against the created order. While male and female together reflect the divine image, homosexuals mirror themselves (the same sex), not God. Homosexuals cannot reproduce or multiply to fulfill the divine mandate. In contrast, equality of women and men reflects the divine intention of Genesis 1:26–27. See my thorough, lengthy discussion of these matters published elsewhere.[7]

(2) Does not the equality of women meet the agenda of feminism and lead to an improper view of the nature of God, as feminine? The answer is that the two are not necessarily related. There is no such Scriptural attestation that parallels what we find in Galatians 3:28. Our concern is to interpret Scripture in the community of faith.

(3) Does not the analogy with the Sabbath fail, since the Sabbath is an Old Testament institution, whereas distinctive roles for men and women are based in both Old Testament and New Testament revelation? In other words, by what authority may we move beyond the teaching of the New Testament regarding roles? Must not its definition of roles, even if reflecting culture and historical (existential) reality, prevail? The answer is that it is by the teaching authority of the Holy Spirit that the Church would come to "new" truth. This is what Jesus promised (John 14:26), John promised (1 John 2:26–27), and what the church has practiced. Jesus paved the way for the changing observance of the Sabbath in light of His bringing in a new era.

For example, in coming to define the limits of the canon, the church was led by the Spirit. There was not a prophetic pronouncement; and there was no apostolic source to cite to define the limits of the canon. The church collectively decided on the basis of the best evidence it had what books should be included in the New Testament canon. It did not come to final resolution of this matter until late in the fourth century. Even with this the Roman Catholic Church later opened up the Old Testament canon at the Council of Trent and accepted eleven of the fourteen apocryphal books from the LXX (the Septuagint or Greek translation of the Old Testament) as part of their Old Testament canon. The Eastern Church has another variation of the canon, holding that the LXX is fully inspired and authoritative.

Another example is the problem of whether Gentiles had to become Jews (that the men had to be circumcised) in order to become Christians. There was no text from the Old Testament Scriptures that the early church could cite, but by mutual prayer and consent the church believed that the Holy Spirit was leading them to conclude that Gentiles did not have to become Jews in order to become God's people (read Acts 15 and Galatians 2).

(4) How does the actualizing of the essential reality of women play out? Is there to be no subordination between husband and wife, or in the church? It means that there is growing equality in the marriage relationship, as each in it yields to their essential oneness in Christ. Wives also love, and husbands also submit. There is mutual submission (Ephesians 5:21). Yet every marriage will differ from the other, due to the differing commitment to, and ability to meet, such a reality of oneness.

In the church, the same variety will prevail, from one local church to another. In some, women may even assume the office of elder or pastor (mission fields, Africa, and the Far East are often clear illustrations of this). The point is that equality of roles is not being mandated or legislated. It will differ according to what each culture and each local situation will bear, accompanied with cautious reflection on the wider impact of the decision.

(5) Should Christians pray that change take place in culture to allow greater freedom for women? It is interesting that Paul does not pray that customs be changed, nor does he ask believers to pray that customs would change, so that greater equality between men and women would prevail. His prayers for the most part concern essential reality—how Christians might grow and witness, how they might attain to greater maturity in their spiritual understanding, etc. Yet he is thoroughly convinced that equality in Christ will eventually impact culture (note 1 Corinthians 7:21: "if you can gain your freedom, do so"; Galatians 3:28; Colossians 3:11).

As Jesus instructed, the people of the kingdom are the saviors of society (the salt and light of the world—Matthew 5:13–16). His kingdom has been forcefully advancing (Matthew 11:12). The gates of hell will not be able to withstand the onward progress of his church (Matthew 16:18). The kingdom of God is to be actualized more and more, that is, further, not just farther, and with its realization the essential realities will be actualized in daily living more and more.

Christians serve both as catalysts for change and conservators of culture. *When* they should do *which* is the nub of the issue. Culture, Scripture, and the reality of essential equality in Christ (theology) must all come together. Remember the principle: *The sooner and wider the giving up of freedom occurs, the sooner and wider the realization of freedom follows.*

A FINAL WORD

So I return to where I began. The Chinese student should not put on a veil or covering because in our culture in America women do not wear veils in public gatherings. The present tense of the command in 1 Corinthians 11:6 has the force: "Keep on wearing the veil" (as culture expects it). It is not an aorist command: "Put on the veil." It is as much a violation of Paul's meaning for Christians to start wearing veils where in the culture women do not wear them as for women to stop wearing veils in cultures where women do wear them.

So what if the culture changes? Then the customs of Christians should change with it, as long as moral issues are not involved. All is to be done for the advancement of the kingdom of Christ to the greater glory of God.

ENDNOTES

1. Liefeld, *Timothy*, 105, says that "public behavior" is the common thread to all these areas, and points to the words that believers might "lead quiet and peaceful lives in all godliness and dignity" from 1 Timothy 2:2 (see similar concerns in Titus 2:4–5, 6–8, 9–10).

2. According to Barrett, *Corinthians*, 333, Calvin asserts that the matters in 14:33–34 are "indifferent, neither good nor bad," and are forbidden only because "they work against seemliness and edification."

3. The exceptions are those things which are physically unchangeable for now—sexual differentiation, the bearing of children, parenting, etc. Schreiner, "Interpretation," 109, acknowledges that differing roles will be terminated in the coming age. In "Head Coverings, Prophecies and the Trinity," in *Recovering Biblical Manhood and Womanhood*, edited by John Piper and Wayne Grudem (Wheaton: Crossway, 1991), 137, Schreiner appropriately acknowledges that people "can be equal in essence and yet have different functions." He points out that 1 Corinthians 11:11–12 makes it clear that women are not inferior to men, nor are they lesser human beings. Blomberg, *1 Corinthians*, 218–19, observes that, on the one hand, Galatians 3:28 should not be applied too broadly, so as to remove all role differentiation or hierarchy; but on the other hand, Paul means more than equality before God for salvation. The Church should "seek outward, public signs in every culture to affirm the full equality of the sexes—and also of races and classes."

One or two questions are pertinent. If the Fall had never happened, would women be barred from spiritually leading or instructing others, including men, in a local assembly of worshippers? Would they not share this role equally with men? Yet the Fall has happened; but so has the transformation that Christ has begun. The standards, values, and ways (of the unseen reality) of the future era have been inaugurated. Is the equal exercise of authoritative teaching roles part of this, to be progressively actualized now?

4. An example of the Spirit's leading the Church is the development of para-church ministries, including institutions such as seminaries, Bible schools, camps, Christian schools, organizations of every stripe, denominations including those with hierarchical structures, etc., and mass communication of the gospel. Paul could not have anticipated our modern era that allows the gospel to go to the world instantly via television, radio, email, internet, cell phone, printing, copying, computer, text messaging, etc. Is it inappropriate for women to use any of these media to "teach authoritatively" the world-wide Church or part of it? Does not the world-wide Church have an enlarged responsibility to discern truth?

5. The result of my paradigm—leading to full equality—is virtually the same result of an approach presented by John G. Stackhouse, Jr., *Finally Feminist: A Pragmatic Christian Understanding of Gender* (Grand Rapids: Baker, 2005). His paradigm centers around the key question (49): What will best advance the kingdom of God? His paradigm includes the principles of (1) equality and (2) the priority of the gospel. He discusses the issues of God's accommodation to human failing, pragmatism, and eschatology ("already but not yet") (42ff.). He points to four intertwining principles (49): gift, calling, order, and edification. He shows that patterns of doubleness (statements supporting both egalitarian and complementary views) recur throughout the Old Testament and the New Testament (64–66). He then responds to arguments used to oppose egalitarianism or feminism—arguments from theology, church history, and contemporary experience and practice (75–97). He presents four principles to guide egalitarianism (97): activism, realism, vocation, and hope. In his first appendix, he gives three ways on how not to decide about gender (105–13): biblicism, cultural conformity or nonconformity, and intuition. His second appendix (115–29) discusses the issue of using inclusive language in translations and in theology, for God. Overall, Stackhouse gives a refreshing approach to the topic and is similar to mine in many ways. He also concludes that both sides are both wrong and right. My paradigm directly appeals to worldview and is applicable to all questions and issues.

6. "Progressive and Historic: The Hermeneutics of 1 Timothy 2:9–

15," in *Women in the Church: An Analysis and Application of 1 Timothy 2:9–15*, edited by Andreas J. Kostenberger and Thomas R. Schreiner, 2nd ed. (Grand Rapids: Baker, 2005), 142.

7. *Homosexuality: Contemporary Claims Examined in Light of the Bible and Other Ancient Literature and Law* (Grand Rapids: Kregel, 2000).

Bibliography

Alford, Henry. *The Greek Testament*. 4 vols. Chicago: Moody, 1958.

Arichea, Daniel and Howard A. Hatton. *Paul's Letters to Timothy and Titus*. New York: United Bible Societies, 1995.

Barrett, C. K. *A Commentary on the First Epistle to the Corinthians*. New York: Harper & Row, 1968.

Bernard, J. H. *The Pastoral Epistles*. Cambridge: University Press, 1906.

Blomberg, Craig. *1 Corinthians: The NIV Application Commentary*. Grand Rapids: Zondervan, 1994.

Bock, Darrell. "Use of the Old Testament in the New." In *Foundations for Biblical Interpretation*. Edited by David S. Dockery, *et al*. Nashville: Broadman & Holman, 1994.

Bruce, F. F. *1 and 2 Corinthians*. London: Oliphants, 1971.

Clark, Elizabeth A. *Women in the Early Church*. Wilmington: Michael Glazier, 1983.

Clement. *1 Clement. The Apostolic Fathers*. Translated by Kirsopp Lake. Loeb Classical Library. Cambridge: Harvard, rep. 1965.

Collins, Raymond F. *First Corinthians*. Collegeville, MN: Liturgical Press, 1999.

Conzelmann, Hans. *1 Corinthians*. Translated by James W. Leitch. Philadelphia: Fortress, 1975.

De Young, James B. and Sarah L. Hurty. *Beyond the Obvious: Discover the Deeper Meaning of Scripture*. Gresham, OR: Vision House, 1995.

De Young, James B. *Homosexuality: Contemporary Claims Examined in Light of the Bible and Other Ancient Literature and Law*. Grand Rapids: Kregel, 2000.

Dibelius, Martin and Hans Conzelmann. *The Pastoral Epistles*. Translated by Philip Buttolph and Adela Yarbro. Edited by Helmut Koester. Philadelphia: Fortress, 1972.

Doriani, Daniel M. *Women and Ministry: What the Bible Teaches*. Wheaton: Crossway, 2003.

Ellicott, Charles J. *St Paul's First Epistle to the Corinthians*. London: Longemans, Green, and Co., 1887.

———. *The Pastoral Epistles*. 3rd edition. London: Longman, Green, Longman, Roberts & Green, 1864.

Fairbairn, Patrick. *Pastoral Epistles*. Minneapolis: James & Klock, rep. 1976.

Fee, Gordon D. *The First Epistle to the Corinthians*. Grand Rapids: Eerdmans, 1987.

Garland, David E. *1 Corinthians*. Grand Rapids: Baker, 2003.

Guthrie, Donald. *The Pastoral Epistles*. Grand Rapids: Eerdmans, 1990.

Hanson, A. T. *The New Century Bible Commentary: The Pastoral Epistles*. Grand Rapids: Eerdmans, 1982.

Hays, Richard B. *First Corinthians*. Louisville: John Knox, 1997.

Hendriksen, William. *New Testament Commentary: Exposition of the Pastoral Epistles*. Grand Rapids: Baker, 1957.

Hurley, James B. *Man and Woman in Biblical Perspective*. Eugene: Wipf and Stock, 2002.

Huther, Joh. Ed. *Critical and Exegetical Hand-Book to the Epistles to Timothy and Titus*. Edited by Timothy Dwight. Winona Lake: Alpha Publications, rep. 1979.

Johnson, Luke Timothy. *The First and Second Letters to Timothy*. *The Anchor Bible*. New York: Doubleday, 2001.

Johnson, S. Lewis. "Role Distinctions in the Church: Galatians 3:28." In *Recovering Biblical Manhood and Womanhood*. Edited by John Piper and Wayne Grudem. Wheaton: Crossway, 1991.

Josephus. *Against Apion*. Translated by H. St. J. Thackeray. Loeb Classical Library. Cambridge: Harvard, rep. 1966.

Josephus. *Antiquity of the Jews: Flavius Josephus Against Apion*. In William Whiston, *Josephus: Complete Works*. Grand Rapids: Kregel, rep. 1966.

Keener, Craig S. *The Bible Background Commentary: New Testament*. Downers Grove: InterVarsity, 1993.

Kelly, J. N. D. *Commentary on the Pastoral Epistles*. London: Adam & Charles Black, 1963.

Knight, George W., III. *The Pastoral Epistles*. *The New International Greek Testament Commentary*. Grand Rapids: Eerdmans, 1992.

Kroeger, Catherine. "Women in Greco-Roman World and Judaism." *Dictionary of New Testament Background.* Edited by Craig A. Evans and Stanley E. Porter. Downers Grove: InterVarsity, 2000.

Lefkowitz, Mary R. and Maureen B. Fant. *Women's Life in Greece & Rome: A Source Book in Translation.* Baltimore: Johns Hopkins, 1982.

Liddon, H.P. *Explanatory Analysis of St. Paul's First Epistle to Timothy.* Minneapolis: Klock and Klock, rep. 1978.

Liefeld, Walter L. *1 and 2 Timothy: The NIV Application Commentary.* Grand Rapids: Zondervan, 1999.

Lock, Walter. *A Critical and Exegetical Commentary on the Pastoral Epistles.* Edinburgh: T & T Clark, 1966.

Mare, W. Harold. *1 Corinthians. The Expositor's Bible Commentary.* Grand Rapids: Zondervan, 1976.

Marshall, I. Howard. *A Critical and Exegetical Commentary on the Pastoral Epistles.* Edinburgh: T & T Clark, 1999.

Merkle, Benjamin L. "Paul's Argument from Creation in 1 Corinthians 11:8–9 and 1 Timothy 2:13–14: An Apparent Inconsistency Answered." *JETS* 49/3 (Sept. 2006) 527–48.

Moo, Douglas. "What Does It Mean Not to Teach or Have Authority Over Men?: 1 Timothy 2:11–15." In *Recovering Biblical Manhood and Womanhood.* Edited by John Piper and Wayne Grudem. Wheaton: Crossway, 1991.

Moore, Russell D. "After Patriarchy, What? Why Egalitarians Are Winning the Gender Debate." *JETS* 49/3 (Sept. 2006) 569–76.

Mounce, William D. *Pastoral Epistles.* Nashville: Nelson, 2000.

Oden, Thomas C. *First and Second Timothy and Titus: Interpretation.* Louisville: John Knox, 1989.

Osborne, Grant R. *The Hermeneutical Spiral.* Downers Grove: InterVarsity, 1991.

Payne, Philip B. *Man and Woman, One in Christ: An Exegetical and Theological Study of Paul's Letters.* Grand Rapids: Zondervan, 2009.

———. "1 Timothy 2.12 and the Use of ουδε to Combine Two Elements to Express a Single Idea." *NTS* 54/2 (April 2008) 235–53.

Quinn, Jerome D. and William C. Wacker. *The First and Second Letters to Timothy.* Grand Rapids: Eerdmans, 2000.

Robertson, Archibald Thomas. *Word Pictures in the New Testament.* Volume 4: *The Epistles of Paul.* Nashville: Broadman, 1931.

Schreiner, Tomas R. "An Interpretation of 1 Timothy 2:9–15." In *Women in the Church: An Analysis and Application of 1 Timothy 2:9–15.* Edited by Andreas J. Kostenberger and Thomas R. Schreiner. 2nd edition. Grand Rapids: Baker Academic, 2005.

———. "Head Coverings, Prophecies and the Trinity: 1 Corinthians 11:2–16." In *Recovering Biblical Manhood and Womanhood.* Edited by John Piper and Wayne Grudem. Wheaton: Crossway, 1991.

Stackhouse, John G., Jr. *Finally Feminist: A Pragmatic Christian Understanding of Gender.* Grand Rapids: Baker, 2005.

Stark, Rodney. *The Rise of Christianity: How the Obscure, Marginal Jesus Movement Became the Dominant Religious Force in the Western World in a Few Centuries.* San Francisco: Harper, 1977.

Sumner, Sarah. "Forging a Middle Way between Complementarians and Egalitarians." In *Women, Ministry and the Gospel: Exploring New Paradigms.* Edited by Mark Husbands and Timothy Larsen. Downers Grove: IVP Academic, 2007.

Thiselton, Anthony C. *The First Epistle to the Corinthians.* Grand Rapids: Eerdmans, 2000.

Towner, Philip H. *The Letters to Timothy and Titus.* Grand Rapids: Eerdmans, 2006.

White, Newport J. D. *The First and Second Epistles to Timothy and the Epistle to Titus.* Volume 4 in *The Expositor's Greek Testament.* Grand Rapids: Eerdmans, 1967.

Witherington, Ben. *Conflict and Community in Corinth.* Grand Rapids: Eerdmans, 1993.

Yarbrough, Robert W. "Progressive and Historic: The Hermeneutics of 1 Timothy 2:9–15." In *Women in the Church: An Analysis and Application of 1 Timothy 2:9–15.* Edited by Andreas J. Kostenberger and Thomas R. Schreiner. 2nd edition. Grand Rapids: Baker, 2005.

Made in the USA
Coppell, TX
30 June 2020

29843427R00075